HOW TO BE
A 6 STAR
BUSINESS

BEYOND
PUBLISHING

New York | Los Angeles | London | Sydney

ISBN Hardcover: 978-1-637922-02-6

ISBN Softcover: 978-1-637922-01-9

TABLE OF CONTENTS

INTRODUCTION

When it comes to superhero films, origin stories are often the most intriguing.

We watch the characters we think we know evolve into who they really are, shining a light, ironically, onto what it means to be human.

And whilst we are no superheroes, with the help and support of some incredible and inspiring humans, we've achieved what feels like a superhuman feat and got this first volume of our book series into your hands.

Thank you for believing in us and buying it.

Yet - what you see now is not at all where we thought of going when '6 Star Business' started.

The origin was an almost throwaway question during a weekly catch-up call between us in September 2020, "Why are 5 stars the most you can rate anything? It doesn't matter if it's a podcast, app, restaurant, business, hotel... 5 stars is always the limit."

Followed by, "If a 6th star was available, what would the business have to be like to get it?"

That conversation has led to a series of divinely timed events, people showing up at the right time, culminating in a podcast that launched with a bang and hasn't stopped since. We've had these stimulating, emotional and insightful conversations with over one hundred people on the 6 Star Business Podcast to date, where we've explored avenues, roads, trails and rabbit holes of personal and business excellence.

Always answering and pondering around, "What does it take to be 6 Star?"

It's evolved into a thriving 6 Star Business Community.

And it is now responsible for this collaborative, co-created 'How to Be a 6 Star Business - Vol 1' book.

In this book, you'll find stories, inspiration, and the genius of 22 entrepreneurs from around the world who provide insights and action steps to go BEYOND the everyday in your business and life - in pursuit of 6 Star excellence.

What is a 6 Star Business?

The model below was co-created by members of the 6 Star Business Community and provides a guide to the pillars and principles of a 6 Star Business that you'll find explored in this book -

If you resonate with any aspect of this model, then you'll love what's coming in the chapters ahead.

The Entrepreneurs who have collaborated with us and provided their 6 Star genius have peeled back the layers and provided a vulnerable and genuine insight into what it means to be 6 Star.

This is not a 'quick fix' or' twelve-point-action-plan' kind of book. Instead, the guidance and wisdom contained in this book are universal and can be adopted whenever you're ready and in whatever order is required. This is a 'choose your own adventure' kind of story.

So please sit back, turn off your phone, get your popcorn ready, and be open to the spotlight shining on you as the Superhero in the centre of this book.

Thanks for being on the ride with us.

We are so excited for the future and that you're coming with us.

Love Ave & Pete
#be6star

CHAPTER ONE

BEING A 6 STAR BUSINESS STARTS WITH YOU

Since we started the 6 Star Business podcast just a few short months ago, one of the more exciting themes we've noticed weaving through is that having a '6 Star Business' starts with being a '6 Star Human'.

Now, this is different from an understanding that we are all 10/10, all of the time.

When a rose seed is planted in the ground, it's 10/10 - and has the capacity for growth.

When the rose seed has sprouted, it's 10/10 - and has the capacity for growth.

When the rose seed becomes a seedling, it's 10/10 - and has the capacity growth.

You get the picture!

Being 6 Star speaks to growth.

Here are six ways you can be 6 Star now:

1. MEDITATE

Of the many scientifically proven benefits of meditation, three are particularly pertinent to being a 6 Star Business.

Meditation increases empathy

Kindness or compassion meditation activates neural connections to brain areas that control good emotions, such as empathy and compassion. The profound state of flow that meditation produces strengthens social relationships and makes us more loving and amiable as individuals.

It's no coincidence that the words 'kindness' and 'love' have been said many times by many different guests on the 6 Star Business podcast.

Meditation improves emotional health and well-being

Meditation has been proven in studies to enhance self-image and self-worth. When we meditate, we get a clear image of our mind and become aware of the thoughts that drive our emotions and behaviours in the present moment.

A large-scale research study found that daily meditation lowers the risk of acquiring depression and mood-related illnesses (Jain, Walsh, Eisendrath, Christensen, & Cahn, 2015). In addition, the study showed that certain kinds of meditation activities that encourage positive thinking might also enhance an individual's overall emotional health.

Meditation enhances cognition

Researchers agree that incorporating meditation into one's daily routine is an excellent way for professionals to increase their chances of success. According to research, both transcendent and mindful meditation practices improve the brain's problem-solving and decision-making strategies, resulting in a positive shift in our professional lives.

2. BE AN 80/20 THINKER

In 1896 the Italian economist Pareto showed that 80% of the land in Italy was owned by 20% of the population. This relationship between cause and consequence, commonly referred to as the Pareto or 80/20 Principle, asserts that a minority of causes, inputs or efforts usually lead to a majority of the results, outputs or rewards. And it has been validated in many areas of business.

20% of products or services usually account for about 80% of total sales value; so do 20% of customers. So, 20% of products or customers usually also account for about 80% of an organisation's profits.

As Richard Koch says in his seminal book, 'The 80/20 Principle: The Secret of Achieving More with Less',

"To engage in 80/20 thinking, we must constantly ask ourselves: what is the 20% that is leading to 80%? We must never assume that we automatically know what the answer is, but take some time to think creatively about it. What are the vital few inputs or causes, as opposed to the trivial many? Where is the haunting melody being drowned by the background noise?"

With practice, 80/20 Thinking allows us to spot the few significant things that are happening and ignore the mass of unimportant things. It teaches us to see the wood for the trees.

This is of profound importance in being a 6 Star Business. It focuses your attention on where any change will have the biggest impact.

3. GET MORE SLEEP

As with meditation, three of the many scientifically proven benefits of sleep are especially relevant to being a 6 Star Business.

Improved mental health

Sleep deprivation is strongly associated with all mental health disorders, particularly depression and anxiety.

"When you find depression or anxiety, 80 to 90% of the time, you'll find a sleep problem." - Brad Wolgast, University of Delaware psychologist

Nota and Coles discovered a link between lower sleep duration and increased OCD symptoms and negative thoughts in a 2015 scientific study of 100 students.

And in the UK, researchers discovered that sleep-deprived individuals were seven times more likely to feel powerless and five times more likely to feel lonely.

Improved concentration and productivity

Sleep is essential for various aspects of brain function. This includes cognition, concentration, productivity, and performance.

All of these are negatively affected by sleep deprivation.

On the other hand, good sleep improves problem-solving skills and enhances the memory performance of both children and adults.

Improved social interactions

Sleep loss reduces your ability to interact socially. Several studies have confirmed this using emotional facial recognition tests.

One study found that people who hadn't slept had a reduced ability to recognise expressions of anger and happiness.

Researchers believe that poor sleep affects your ability to recognise important social cues and process emotional information.

4. BE A TIME MAGICIAN

Whilst it's true that everyone has the same amount of 'physical', chronological time of twenty-four hours/1,440 minutes/86,400 seconds available to them every day, there are those among us who appear able to manipulate time. These people can achieve more than seems possible in the same amount of time we have.

Their secret?

A different mindset.

Here's the mindset of these time wizards when faced with a new task:

1. Does this task even have to be done? Can it be eliminated?

2. If it can't be eliminated, can it be automated?

3. If it can't be automated, can it be delegated?

4. If it can't be delegated, does it have to be done now?

5. If it does, give yourself permission to focus on it. If not, put it on hold until you're ready to let it start again at step 1.

(The above is courtesy of Rory Vaden, and he calls people with this mindset Time Multipliers.)

Why is this important for being a 6 Star Business? Because the more time you can free up for yourself, the more time you'll have for 80/20 Thinking (see above), which will result in an exponential payback for yourself and your business.

5. BE IN COMMUNITY

Any meaningful endeavour in any aspect of life is challenging and requires us to adapt and grow; develop new skills and improve old ones; go where we've never gone before - physically, mentally and emotionally.

Jim Rohn said, "Everyone should strive to be a millionaire. Not for the money in the bank but for who you have to become in the process."

And we say, "Business is the ideal playground for personal development."

So, you may not realise it, but the real reason you started your business was to accelerate your transformation as a human!

And that journey of transformation, like any journey, is both more likely and more fun when you're with others on the same journey.

So, if you're not in a community of business owners who are on the same wavelength as you, find one and or create one.

6. BE ON PURPOSE

We have saved the most important for last.

By definition, a 6 Star Business is a purpose-driven business, and the ideal is to express the purpose of your business in a single sentence of fewer than ten words.

A clearly defined, articulated and lived-out purpose will attract the kind of employees, partners and customers that make being a 6 Star Business almost inevitable.

And on that note, read on for Aveline's vulnerable and powerful chapter on the importance of finding and using your purpose in business.

CHAPTER TWO

THE IMPORTANCE OF FINDING AND USING YOUR PURPOSE IN BUSINESS

"I'm not ready to be a father."

The words landed like large bricks falling on my heart and reverberated as loudly as if they dropped from a twelve-story ledge onto the pavement below. In that moment and many more to follow, I realised how incredibly alone I was and how irrevocably my world had changed. Yet in the middle of that vast space of loneliness shone a tiny flame of warmth, like a guiding light showing me where to go and that I was going to have this baby, regardless.

Was I crazy? Perhaps on the outside, I was. None of my friends was married yet or had children, and I'd held a baby once for about two minutes. I was living at home at the time, and I had no support from my 'now ex' or his family. So was it even logical to go ahead with this pregnancy? I was completely open to my potential outcomes and choices and wasn't afraid of any of them. All of them had been suggested to me, of course, by my ex and my friends. In that 'lack of fear,' I allowed something to come into my awareness that wasn't coming from my mind or rational thought.

I clearly recall a moment when I was sitting on some stairs outside of the apartment after my ex had delivered his deafening words when I heard the first whispers of this 'knowing' inside. I couldn't quite identify it at the time, yet it felt strong, caring, and wise, so I permitted myself to listen to it further.

This was the moment that changed everything for me. It was the beginning of a journey of learning to 'tune into' my inner knowing and be pulled and guided by that. I had new feelings about parenting, who I was as a human, and what was important to me. It ignited in me a drive and intention to be ready for this child to arrive and be a powerful, strong and successful parent – despite my loud critics, having no partner and absent family support. Listening to that 'inner knowing' was one of the most critical and pivotal decisions I have ever made.

The trust I placed in myself that day sitting on the steps outside the apartment is the same trust I have today when I work with clients and help them recognise and use theirs as they search for their purpose and reason for being in business.

What's genuinely devastating is that most business owners don't even know how important it is to be tapped into their purpose and drive their business with it. Just to be clear, being driven by your purpose isn't only crucial for business owners! It's something everyone should be tuning into, so they can live an inspired life filled with meaning and joy instead of confusion and emptiness.

For a business to make the most impact and be 6 Star, the owner needs to align with their true purpose.

Finding your Purpose

So how do we 'tap into' our purpose? To be frank, that could take an entire book to explain its detailed entirety. So my simplified version is this:

1. Create some mental and physical space for yourself that's 100% free of distractions. Then turn off your phone!

2. Brainstorm with pen and paper, or on a whiteboard, what's meaningful to you – and list out all the reasons why. Keep going until you can't think of anything else.

3. Look for patterns and similarities: where are they?

4. Ask yourself how important this really is to you?

5. Ask yourself: is there something I'd like to see change or happen that's related to this that would energise me and excite me to no end? Where's the change I want to see?

6. If you could describe that intention or outcome in just five-ten words, what would it be?

That's a start. This work takes patience, space, and the ability to listen to yourself inside and ask yourself more profound questions.

Think of your purpose as an energetic thread that connects you through all your experiences, from now until the end of your life. Imagine there's a current running through that is bi-directional yet is always pulling you towards your purpose. Just as the ocean's waves can pull you up and over in the short term, their overall intention is to reach the high tide or the low tide. In, out, back, forth. Your purpose current works the same way, yet your 'high tide' is at a point in time that's unknown.

Why? Because we have no idea how long it will take, and the reality is we may never achieve it in our lifetime! Remember, your true purpose comes from inside of you; it's spiritual, a knowing; a feeling; and a recognition of what fuels you. If you don't resonate with the word 'spiritual', then use another word that describes your deeper connection to the part of you that's still talking to you when the rest of the world is quiet.

When Your Purpose isn't Clear

It's not bad or wrong to have no idea about what your purpose is; it just makes life that much harder to live each day if you don't! I've worked with many clients who aren't driven by a purpose and focus only on making money. Compared to those driven by a purpose, those without a purpose were more stressed, uptight, and had less joy in their lives.

Those driven by a purpose were fun to be around, made better decisions that reaped better results, had more 'coincidental' positive events happen and achieved their goals more easily. For example, my client Megan continually told me that she knew her purpose and had successfully embedded it throughout her business.

Yet her results showed otherwise, and when I asked her to tell me what it was, she gave me a different answer each time. This lack of clarity results in the purpose having less impact and less power. So, I convinced her to do a session with me, and she did so reluctantly. I took her through the process, and she burst into tears unexpectedly when she finally realised her purpose. Her delight and relief were audible as she exclaimed, "OMG, Aveline!" and shortly after that was able to see how to embed her purpose throughout her business.

My experiences have shown me that people will tune into their purpose when the time is right for them, and not a moment sooner. I believe that everyone has a purpose, yet not everyone gets out of their mind for long enough to listen to what it is.

The Power of Having a Purpose in your Business

Hopefully, by now, you can understand the power of living 'on purpose' and why it's so important. When we take our purpose and apply it to our business, one of two things can happen:

1. We realise we're in the wrong business!

2. Our business takes on a whole new life and meaning.

If you fall into the first category, this is exciting: it's an opportunity to get out and find a new business that aligns with you and your purpose. Reaching this level of clarity is a gift, as it will save you a lot of wasted time staying in a business that doesn't align with you. A telling sign that this is the case is an internal feeling of relief.

If you fall into the second category, this can be a pivotal turning point in your business life cycle and your life in general.

For example, here's how this played out for a client, John, who started working with me when his business had been going for 12 years quite successfully. However, he was bored and disengaged with his customers. So he had started to created side hustle projects that weren't going anywhere fast. Although he didn't understand the value of identifying his purpose, he accepted the idea. As soon as we'd uncovered his purpose and how his business aligned with it, John became reinvigorated, his passion revived, and he was supercharged on his path again.

Purpose and 6 Star Businesses

I've asked dozens of successful business owners what being 6 Star means to them, and the resounding response is that it's a 6th dimension that comes from inside the owner, the employees, the people. It's a connection between the mind, the heart, and the recipient of that action. It's not about following a '7 step process to success' or focussing only on boosting profits! In fact, several highly successful long-term entrepreneurs candidly stated (in various ways):

> *"You can't reach 6 stars unless you're connected to your purpose. Without purpose, you'll only be 5 stars at best."*

There are entrepreneurs I meet who tell me they are purpose-driven. When I ask them to share their purpose with me, they start talking about everything that is meaningful to them, covering different topics and sometimes don't stop talking for over two minutes! I then ask them to sum it up in one sentence, and this also proves difficult! But, there's no denying their internal drive, passionate pursuits and the things that give them meaning.

However, until they've narrowed down their purpose in a way that succinctly sums it up and articulates it in a concise sentence, it just sounds like a lot of words without one clear intention. Therefore, the less clear and concise you are about your purpose, the less impactful you're going to be in bringing it about. Your purpose has the most power when it's clear, concise, meaningful, and you can express it in less than ten words.

Twenty-Two Years Later

It's been twenty-two years since that day when I sat on the steps outside the apartment and listened to my inner voice, which resulted in me going into parenthood alone. It was a life-altering moment for many reasons, not the least of which was when I trusted in my inner voice and found a greater reason for being.

I've been pulled by that magical cord of purpose, bringing me to where I am today, helping other people honour their purpose in business and life. I know how powerful it is to live 'on purpose' and its impact on people.

To sum up, "What would it be like if every business was driven by a purpose, bigger than themselves, that reached the far-flung corners of their existence?"

AVELINE CLARKE

Aveline is known for activating people's true purpose in business and aligning that with the entire customer journey.

She has vast experience mapping, creating and building customer journeys using principles of human behaviour and clever marketing automation technology. Her business, Journey Point, helps create these redefined journeys so that businesses can go to market with the most engaging and effective messaging to 'PULL' the market towards them and create the optimum experience for their customers.

She is the co-founder of the 6 Star Business movement, which includes the Podcast, Community and the Book.

She is a partner of One Earth – an entrepreneur education school – helping businesses to grow successfully.

Aveline is passionate about growth, education, health, creating positive experiences and helping people become the best versions of themselves to contribute to the positive evolution of the world. She also enjoys nature, the ocean, spending time with her children, and exploring new places when she can.

You can contact Aveline via:

Website: https://www.journeypoint.com.au/meet-aveline/

LinkedIn: linkedin.com/in/avelineclarke

Instagram: https://instagram.com/avelineclarke

CHAPTER THREE

WHY YOUR PHILANTHROPIC MINDSET IS CAUSING YOUR BUSINESS TO FAIL

"If charity cost nothing,
the world would be full of philanthropists."
- Proverb

Angela: *"When I first left the corporate world, I had no idea about how to value myself or my services - or even what those services were. I knew how to package up day rates and negotiate a salary for a new role. But I didn't know how to value what I had to offer independently; without the 'big brand' banner of my previous corporate life.*

Self-doubts creep in. You worry about whether people will see the value in what you offer as a small business or independent specialist or whether you might lose customers by raising prices.

It was easier to stay attached to the far away altruistic ideals of wanting to make an impact.

The truth was that the fear of failure prevented me from seeing the bigger picture.

As I watched my savings dwindle over the months and with the business making much less what I earned in my corporate days, I realised that I would need a mindset switch to make it.

After many conversations with my best friend and now business partner Cristina, we realised that moving from selling time to selling VALUE through a well-packaged offer would be the starting point of that switch.

And overcoming the mental hurdle of pricing it at the right value."

Best friends since we were fifteen; we are now in our late thirties and run **Grow Your Brand With Impact**, a marketing firm that we are building into our empire.

Our long-term vision is to create a world of resilient individuals empowered through knowledge and support to carve out their unique path to economic success.

A big mission indeed...

But to do that we would need to make serious money!

Switch in mindset

Cristina: *"I think I'm going to pitch our offer at USD 5000."*

Angela: *"Are you crazy! Who is going to pay that? Our clients don't have that kind of money! They come to us for help to make money. They need clients ASAP, as they are running out of money."*

Cristina: *"But Ange, think of what you used to charge for your time and expertise. We are only asking what it's worth, and if our clients can't see that, are they the right clients for us anyway?"*

A few days later…

Cristina: *"So I made a booboo. I said the USD price in pounds by mistake, the client didn't blink, and on top of that said yes, then asked for an invoice to be raised."*

Angela: *"What? Are you serious? He paid?"*

Cristina: "I'm *still processing, my heart is racing, but I guess it means we have validated the higher price."*

People will pay for the value your offer will give them.

There is a reason Chanel handbags and Lamborghinis are sold every day despite much cheaper alternatives available in the market. The question often is, what value do you bring? What value do you give your clients based on your learnings, experience, and expertise?

Running a business is hard. Running a partnership is often harder. Ours works because we see the bigger picture; we want to make an impact and earn lots of money. So how do we ensure that *we can* make a profit?

You need RESOURCES (profit) to make an impact

The expertise industry continues to grow each year, with the coaching and consulting industry alone estimated to be valued at approximately $15B globally pre-covid (econsultancy.uk). And it's estimated to be the second-fastest growing industry globally by PWC.

Covid has only further accelerated this trend - pushing more talented and well-qualified individuals to focus on creating their own securities through their business outside of the corporate world.

Despite this, only 28% of these individuals report earning more than in their previous corporate role.

These numbers highlight a disconnect between what value the industry places on our coaching and consulting expertise and what we value that to be.

To close this gap in your level of success, and most importantly, profits will depend on your ability to scale what you do, stand out as an expert and invest in the right areas to **make money and sustainably grow your business.**

The higher the profit - the greater the impact.

So, where are you now?

Do you find yourself questioning your value?

Do you price your services using a cost vs a value mindset?

Do you discount or lower prices to help someone in need because they 'can't afford it'?

Do you really make an impact by doing those things?

Business success requires several things, and I will focus on four that are critical to business success (achieving profit) and making a difference.

1. VISION

To get somewhere, you need to know your destination.

Your vision and corresponding strategy are some of the essential pieces to spend time getting down on paper before leaping into anything.

This also serves as a holding spot for your bigger ideas and painting the roadmap to get there.

2. STRATEGY

This part consists of 3 elements:

1. A *Profit Vehicle* - this consists of an offer valued correctly to make a profit, building your pool of resources, and the ability to package and sell it beyond your 1:1 time.

2. A *clear market* that wants it, and importantly, values it.

3. A *mechanism* to bring this to market at scale.

Your first goal here is to find that sweet spot invalidating your offer and the value attached (a low price may attract the wrong client, and an overpriced offer may set false expectations).

3. EXECUTION

One of the best pieces of business advice we once received was from a business mentor - and it relates to the childhood fable you may be familiar with of the tortoise and the hare.

"Don't try to be sexy like the speedy hare; the slow and steady (read consistent!) tortoise is the one that will finish the race," he said.

It will take a few attempts to find that unique spot in your market then land the perfect message that will ignite your customer to action.

This is where your best tortoise qualities come into play:

- Consistency.

- Energy conservation and a steady mindset to see it through.

- Belief in that final vision.

Parts 2 & 3 are intimately connected and consist of several components you'll need to get right. So we'll tell you right off the bat, it's will take a few attempts.

You'll also need to be cautious not to linger too long in either strategy or execution.

Strategy is a fun place to be but lingering traps you in an insular bubble of thinking and developing creative ideas, but that bubble is precisely where they stay.

The real test is to put it into execution and in front of customers. But, unfortunately, in our experience, the lag of putting strategy into execution is often about our fears of rejection.

Likewise, jumping straight into execution without first spending the time working through the strategic foundations is a recipe for wasted effort, money down the drain, and disappointment.

Trust us; we've been there!

4. PROFITS

Your number one priority as a business owner must be to generate profits (i.e. resources). Then use your profits to run your business profitably, fund your chosen lifestyle and reinvest to grow your business and create further impact.

Success in making a **philanthropic impact** requires all of these **four things** to be in place.

THEN you need the philanthropic mindset.

BUT that philanthropic mindset itself is not going to go the distance on its own.

Case Study

Let's introduce Richard* - a construction industry mentor who wanted to have a profitable business AND be philanthropic.

Most people view construction workers as loud lads at the pub early in the afternoon nursing a pint of beer - and a few empty ones on the table! But there is much more to this community. They are also often fathers and caretakers of their families, their communities and huge drivers of their local economies.

Richard had seen first-hand the toll of business struggle - mental and physical exhaustion, his family breaking down and not making money in the building world.

He could have easily made an excuse to devalue his price point so his clients could afford it.

Our first hurdle was therefore elevating and positioning the value of his offering accurately.

"Richard, your experience is worth at least three, four, even five times more than that! How are you going to physically handle the clients you need to make your target if you keep your price so low?"

The next hurdle was the process to convert calls to sales.

"I still haven't had any sales calls booked."

"Richard, have you reached out to those guys who had questions from your live session?"

"No, I was waiting for people to book via the automation."

Richard saw my face, *"Ok, go on say it."*

"Richard, don't rely on automation."

Angela was disappointed. A slew of qualified leads coming through the campaign we had helped set up, and not one booked onto a call.

Your business is no one else's responsibility but yours. Indeed, not even the responsibility of your automation.

But thankfully, he did not give up.

While he bungled the first campaign, it was a valuable learning experience, and he determinedly took our advice.

We rode through the second campaign, then three more campaigns together. Each time Richard gained more confidence and persistence, which was rewarded through results.

He did not let a single opportunity slip through by the second campaign and closed at a 40% rate because of persistent follow-up.

EXECUTION, CONSISTENCY and PERSISTENCE

Summary

As a business leader, you get into what you do for a reason.

If you're even reading this book about 6 Star Businesses and this specific chapter - we'll bet it wasn't because you were looking to get rich quickly.

You wanted to make an impact. And you had a burning desire to push yourself out there doing something different because you knew you could make a difference.

Profits are key to making your impact sustainable for you and your business.

Challenge yourself with the question - is altruism holding you back from making money?

Or does a slight fear come into play?

Business success requires several things. Therefore, we focused on four key factors in this chapter - **Vision, Strategy, Execution, and Profits.**

Remember that success in making a philanthropic impact requires **all of the above** to be in place, and THEN the philanthropic mindset.

That philanthropic mindset itself will not go the distance on its own.

So, create your big vision. Start with Step 1. Build your resources. Fund your impact.

Let's go.

*Names changed to protect client's business details

ANGELA TSAI

Angela grew up the eldest child of 3. She lives today in London with her husband and cat.

Having lived in 3 different countries by the age of 12 - she learnt from an early age that *no matter where you are, you have the ability to carve out something for yourself.* She has since made it her mission to help others achieve their own imprints and forever prosper economically.

She set up her first foundation in Amsterdam in 2015, with bigger ambitions to achieve more to empower young women and girls worldwide economically. After leaving the corporate world in 2018 in search of more fulfilment, she founded Grow Your Brand With Impact - a brand & marketing strategy consultancy, where she, her business partner and her team help their clients to unleash their voice and value to the world

CRISTINA CASTRO

Cristina is a truly global citizen, travelling with her partner and her rescue westie dog.

She began her career working with doctors to ensure they understood that their patients were also their clients. Then, following a stint consulting in a charity in the Big Apple, she returned to the sun-filled skies of Sydney, Brisbane and Melbourne.

Cristina moved from there to London, where her journey of discovering philanthropy and business ownership truly begins - as a partner in Grow Your Brand With Impact.

From the corporate glass corner office overlooking Darling Harbour to the sun-soaked skies of Spain and everything in between, Cristina shares her stories of resisting the entrepreneur title due to parental baggage to the ambition of revolutionising the education industry.

***Psst, CC & Angela here. Want a FREE ebook?

Visit https://growyourbrandwithimpact.com/e-book/5keys to grab your copy.

Along with your free ebook, you'll get my latest news and updates, insider exclusives, plus excellent marketing tips and recommendations. It's a lot of fun! Happy reading, :)

You can reach Angela and Cristina via:
Angela Tsai | CEO & Founder
Grow Your Brand With Impact
https://www.linkedin.com/in/angelatsai1

Cristina Castro | Partner
Grow Your Brand With Impact
https://www.linkedin.com/in/cristina-castro-reyes

Website: www.growyourbrandwithimpact.com
Instagram:
https://www.instagram.com/growyourbrandwithimpact
Facebook:
https://www.facebook.com/growyourbrandwithimpact

CHAPTER FOUR

HOW TO DELIVER CHANGE THROUGH A 6 STAR CULTURE

Why is the culture of a business so important? Surely the financials or operations deliver the tangible results and success? This is true, but a toxic culture can kill a company, and a positive culture can grow or revive a business's success.

At thirty-two, I was handed the opportunity of a lifetime because of the hard work I had put into developing a reputation. My personal brand. It was the dream job, big everything, salary, car, corner office. You get the picture.

My job was to revive the business performance and be a Change Manager. Get results no matter what, the 80's approach! I'd never done that before, but how hard could it be? I'd never managed a large team, but I was confident I could pull it off.

Within three months, I realised it wasn't that easy, and I was out of my depth; the harder I tried, the more mistakes I made and successfully alienated everyone from the Managing Director to the tea-boy. Yes, I had a tea-boy. Sadly, people wanted to help me, and I pushed them away.

By the end of twelve months, I was unceremoniously sacked. I wasn't surprised; in fact, I was expecting it.

That wasn't the problem, as I had unbounded hubris. What hurt me was that only a few people came and wished me well. It felt like an emotional dagger stabbing me as the door slammed behind me.

I made a pact with myself that I would never behave like that again and dived into improving myself, what is now called Emotional Intelligence. First, I educated myself by reading the management classics, including Dale Carnegie's *How to Win Friends and Influence People* and Stephen Covey's books. Then, I spoke with as many successful people as I could and sought out Mentors for guidance.

In 2009 I had the opportunity to work in Papua New Guinea to help corporatise a business. Over the next ten years, I rounded off my management skills in human resources and understood how a positive culture is the glue that binds the business's success.

In my last role, my job was as a Change Manager. I had one hundred and twenty staff; my job was to turn the business around.

When I left, the organisation was better than when I found it, and I had treated the staff with respect, which created trust that money could not buy. They were proud of what they had achieved as I had gifted them self-confidence and empowerment. I was proud of them.

There were no emotional daggers this time. On the contrary, we hugged and cried and were equally grateful for the experience.

That is why I do what I do. I want you to experience the power of a cultural transformation and its impact on both the business and the people who work in it.

So how do you deliver and experience this transformation?

Culture Starts with Vulnerability

As a leader, I believe you must be vulnerable, open and honest. Vulnerability is a strength, not a weakness. When you're vulnerable and truthful, it demonstrates that it's OK not to know, be scared, and make mistakes.

It seems too simple, but if you're open, others will eventually be open too.

The people under your charge feel safe to open up. This builds a platform of trust between you, a bond you need to honour. These days it's known as Psychological Safety; I call it caring.

Get Started by Doing Nothing

The mistake I made as a thirty-two-year-old was to start changing things automatically. So, if you're looking to create change, first take your time to understand. Don't be in a hurry to change things for the sake of looking like you're doing something.

Regardless of whether your role is owner, manager or advisor, the first step is to observe. Listening is the key. Remember, you have two ears and one mouth and use them in that proportion. You'll find that few people enjoy change. There will be resistance, so look for signals and the possible saboteur.

Repeating what you've heard confirms you've truly understood the culture and business.

Have a Plan

Having a clear objective and goal is obviously important; communicating this to everyone is even more critical. If you don't tell the staff what's going on, the gossip and rumour mills will explode.

My approach is to look at each functional area and assess where it lies in the "Satisfaction Level" assessment and what shift is needed? How Important and Urgent is making the change? And what resources can you allocate to shifting the needle to the desired Satisfaction Level?

Take a holistic view of how a change in one area impacts another -The Ripple Effect Concept.

You can't change everything, so you need a plan to work out the priorities.

The key here is to include the relevant stakeholders at each stage of the Plan's development. So not only will you uncover their genius and ideas, but you'll also be making a deposit into the Cultural Trust Bank, a real asset on the businesses balance sheet.

Acknowledge Success

The best way to alienate people is to tell them what they've been doing is wrong. Some success was created before you arrived by the existing employees, so you need to honour that. Another deposit into the Cultural Trust Bank! Change for change's sake is not your mantra; change needs to be purposeful and intentional.

The conversation is not what's broken, but what could we do differently to be even better?

These are likely to be difficult conversations, so get them on and off the table as quickly as possible. The stronger your relationship with your team, the easier these become. Regardless of the relationship, the difficult conversations relate to the project's goals, looking forward, not at past mistakes. This provides the context for the conversation.

Understand the Existing Process

Question - "Why do we do it like that?"

Answer - "We've always done it like that," Red Flag.

To paraphrase the words of Michael Gerber in the *Emyth*, if you have a problem, put in a process, and the problem goes away.

This is the least sexy thing you can do when changing an organisation's culture, but it is the operational foundation and must not be overlooked.

Whatever goal you have in place cannot be achieved without this fundamental business principle.

These processes need to support the values of the business, not impede their performance.

Create a Framework of Accountability

People prefer boundaries. It gives them comfort and something to push against as they grow.

It's almost counterintuitive to have boundaries and encourage them to be stretched; nevertheless, a positive culture encourages creativity, pushing boundaries.

Creating a safe place is at the core. Your staff need to know you have their back when things go wrong.

If a team member has failed inside the boundary, find out if they have the skills needed to do the job. Do they have the time and capacity, or are you flogging the willing horse?

If it's a mistake that's outside the boundary, that's a good thing because it indicates a desire to improve. But there is a lack of knowledge or experience.

In both cases, as the leader, acknowledge that your team member failed because of something you have not done. The second is finding what's missing and working on supporting them to fill the gap.

Mistakes are only decisions with not enough information.

Sometimes they have just plain behaved badly. If it's an attitude, it's one of those 'difficult conversations'.

At times like this, you feel disappointed in their behaviour, and your natural reaction is to get angry. But, instead, stop and take the time to understand why they have behaved this way.

The context for the conversation is you "value them and their contribution, but at this moment you are disappointed". You want to understand what has caused this behaviour change. Get this right, and there is another deposit in the Cultural Trust Bank.

Entrepreneurs and founders also need to be held accountable! Having good people around you who are not scared to call out the Boss is the sign of a safe culture.

How Long Does it Take to Build a 6 Star Culture?

The first ninety days is a focus on the foundations.

I don't think there is ever a 'finish line' in building a 6 Star Culture as long as you make more deposits than withdrawals.

Tough Love in the Security Business

Trust and Accountability can be deposits or withdrawals from the Cultural Trust Bank.

I had one occasion where the Cultural Trust funds were leaking out the back door.

I was asked to manage a team of Technicians and Administrators. The business was losing money and had never met budget. My job was Change Manager.

The problem was simple, our pricing was wrong, our systems were non-existent, and our Customer Experience was dreadful. Our Technicians were the worst offenders, not turning up on time, or at all, and doing poor work.

Over time we put in place systems and processes to control our quoting, sales conversions and profit. However, the one thing we were still lagging behind in was the Customer Experience.

We put one simple Accountability Principle in place "Our Word is our Promise."

We had one highly skilled technician who was a law unto themselves and continually refused to abide by our Accountability Principle. He decided he would make up his own rules.

At a toolbox meeting, I said to him, "You have disappointed this customer four times by not turning up as agreed. Is there any reason why it's not been done?"

"I'll do it when I can", he replied. "If you don't like what I do, I'll just leave."

"I accept your resignation," I replied.

There was a stunned silence.

From that moment on, everyone understood that the Accountability Principle was not just words; it was our Culture.

From that moment, the team buzzed with positive energy. Others who had been waiting for an opportunity stepped up. The toxic team member had gone, and they were the real problem.

Cultural Trust Bank deposit.

Summary

To build a positive culture, you need to care. Care about your people, your customers, your suppliers, your community.

Open and honest communication with vulnerability being the first deposit in the Cultural Trust Bank account.

Be patient. It took years to build the existing culture, and it will take time to develop a different culture.

Do the necessary (not sexy) task of putting in place Systems and Processes - all with a purpose.

Be clear on the Culture you want to create. My favourite is Accountability.

Even a great culture can degrade eventually over time so keep working at it!

STEVE SANDOR

Passion and purpose are to make a difference in the lives of others.

Father of four, grandfather, golf nut, motorbike riding enthusiast, and prepared to try anything once, except sky diving!

Steve Sandor uses his over thirty-five years of management experience from a diverse range of industries in Australia and overseas to now supports small business owners in scaling their business. Steve says, "Business is made up of Product, Processes and People, and it's the people part that is the most important component."

Having spent more than 80% of his career managing small and large teams, he understands and appreciates that running and managing a business is simple but not easy and definitely worth the effort when you get it right.

CHAPTER FIVE

COLLABORATION WITH PROFITABILITY

In two years, my business grew from five staff to one hundred and ten staff and achieved a turnover of thirty-million dollars. The pace was dizzying.

The way I did achieved it was to partner with three of my biggest competitors. They were international companies with thousands of staff and multimillion-dollar turnover.

How did I achieve it? Let's go back a bit.

In 2013 I went through a copyright claim challenge over my business name, resulting in me having to rebrand and reposition my business from scratch. Between 2006 and 2013, I had launched my business. During that time, I'd been faced with a corporate takeover of my franchise, loss of that business and then in 2013 received a claim against my trademark application, forcing me to close and rebrand.

I had staff, premises, and commitments, but I didn't have customers - confronting yes, but there were several things in my favour.

I knew the industry, had an automated paperless system and held the licences required. An industry that had complex compliance, and the barrier to entry was significant. Becoming and retaining

RTO status involves complex and costly systems that traditionally are heavy in human resources and paperwork. This meant many RTOs struggled to provide the level of support required to ensure students progressed and completed as they simply did not have the financial or people resources. My systems enabled me to repurpose a team of ten to student support rather than data input.

I knew who the big players were; so, I created a plan. I was a registered training organisation. The government had created funding for individuals looking to up-skill to improve their career prospects, and my organisation could serve them AND get funding from the government if we met their criteria

Being approved for the funding was going to take one to two years. This was too long to wait: my business needed growth and profits now!

I needed a plan to relaunch to support my staff, stakeholders, and my family.

I needed to find a partner amongst my largest competitors. I remember a reference between our companies "the little Orange Speed Boat" and the "Queen Mary".

The Queen Mary were my competitors – refined, large and slow to get moving, rigid in their process, but had a massive following registering more than 50,000 students per annum. I was the orange speed boat – lithe, quick to change direction, agile with sleek processes; however, our load capacity was estimated to be 5,000 registrations per annum.

You might ask what I was thinking, given I was a small business with five staff in a local suburb of Brisbane.

I dared to ask my competitors for a meeting; I was prepared for every question they had and the unexpected. But they continued to listen to me. I've always lived by the phrase – "Have the answer ready before the question is asked".

Other options were available to me, such as going back to the traditional sales process of cold calling, knocking on doors by rebuilding the sales team. Although it was doable, the return on investment was low and slow.

It was going to be difficult, yet I believed in my approach and knew when we secured the agreements, it would support not only the business but my team, family and, most importantly, offer businesses in Australia a new option.

My goal was to provide a product that would help build small businesses and give them the skills and the capability to grow like never before.

The standard in the industry was generic qualifications that were no different from one organisation to the next. As a result, the reputation of the industry was slipping. With poor completion rates, no support, and disgruntled learners, there was only one place to go – up! So I came up with an idea for a unique high-end product.

I knew it was going to be different from every other provider in the country. Whilst it would be the most expensive in the industry, the value add would be of such a high standard and from such a different perspective that I knew would grab my competitor's attention.

I was driven to put a dent in the failure rate of small business in Australia. The only way to do that was to provide a product funded by the government that would take small businesses to a different level.

Upon completion, students would achieve a diploma in business bundled with:

- business & marketing plan,

- website,

- social media strategy,

- accountants' advice, and

- a financial

- plan

Something that was not offered in the education sector.
I had to be strategic.
I had to be clear about what was in it for them, how I would make it easy and what the consequences would be if they didn't partner with me.
I did my homework- I had to know who these companies were, how they worked, and their pain point.

What I discovered was:

- The funding they held depended on their performance.

- If they didn't use it all, they would lose it.

- If they overspent, they would lose it.

- They were not agile.

- They were paper-based

My plan was simple. Make an offer so compelling by addressing these pain points that they couldn't say no.

It was clear from the beginning that I was applying for my funding, and I was looking for a placeholder for up to two years, and once I had my funding, the agreements would end.

Like them, I was a registered training organisation. I had my own systems and knew the complexities of compliance and what it took to maintain it. I knew that their compliance systems were cumbersome, staff heavy and paper-heavy.

My automation removed 90% of the paperwork, and I utilised my team to support the students, not data input. Something never done before in the industry.

Meaning I could achieve and process more enrolments with less staff and at a low error rate.

I didn't need their products and would find my own customers.

I needed their funding, and I knew they had difficulty utilising their funding allocation. This put them at risk of losing their funding pool.

These are the key reasons we succeeded:

We were unexpected

I was prepared; everything was documented with my reasons and intent clear.

No surprises - we documented every process, workflow and script.

We came to the table as though we were already in partnership. Every move that we would make from cold calling, enrolment, induction, training through to completion and reporting was documented, and work flowed.

Our product

No product like this existed in the market.

Our product was priced at five times theirs, and I shared twenty-five percent of my income. This share almost equated to the value of their product – it was a no brainer.

Our endorsements

We secured an endorsement from Tony Robbins to promote our diploma to his audience.

This would enable them again to piggyback off our success to the benefit of their business.

Our systems

We were the first RTO in the country to API our reporting system to our delivery system and our sales system. As a result, my automation reduced the compliance cost from 40% to 10% and our error rate reduced to 5%.

The system was made available to our partners. We were giving them clarity at every step and aspect of the operation.

Sales capacity

The proposed volume of enrolments was 100 students a week. Instead, we achieved 200 students a week.

This volume would ensure that they could utilise all their funding and not oversubscribe their funding.

I was partnering with three competitors and was able to redirect enrolments from one partner to another as I filled the allocation. This capability was unheard of in the industry.

Compliance

Being an accredited RTO gave them the confidence that I understood the importance of the complexity of compliance to ensure that no one would risk losing their licence.

The rigour of my systems and documented processes were better and more efficient than theirs.

Performance

Our completion rate was as high as 85% when the industry standard was as low as 3%.

They could report improved completion rates, thereby securing their funding pool. They could piggyback off my success.

While my story is based on a specific industry with its own complexities and challenges, the learnings I gained from these partnerships are shared below.

There is no glass ceiling

Small business owners need to create bigger, breath-taking goals so they can grow and scale to survive.

The opportunities available to small business today have never been so exciting, accessible and achievable; there is no glass ceiling when you are a 6 Star business.

This is what I learnt:

- Know your industry inside and out.
- Have a proven model building your creditability.
- Know your partner. Understand their pain and create a product that speaks to it but complements their products.
- Make it so easy that they cannot refuse.
- Know what it costs to produce, deliver, and the net profit you aim for – check weekly or at least monthly.
- Share the income.
- Create diversity in your business by either product, partners, or how it's delivered.
- Reduce their risk.
- Give them confidence in your systems. Make the access easy.
- Document everything. Use automation. Let them see how, why and what you're doing.
- Let them manage you until you prove to them that they don't need to anymore.
- Never stop communicating, sharing, and collaborating.
- Pay on time.
- Have the answer ready before the question is asked.

I've always known is that if I want something to change, it is up to me. I've spent my entire career being unexpected.

I'd submit proposals to my manager of ways to do things differently, recommending opportunities. I learned quickly if I did the research and gave a compelling summary of the win-win. It would be rare for me not to succeed.

This translated into business ownership. It is only now, when I look back, that I realise the common thread throughout my story has been this approach.

When you are a 6 Star business, you will be unexpected and memorable.

To be honest, our level of success was unexpected. We knew we had a 6 Star formula, and when we experienced the perpendicular growth, we knew we were onto something incredible.

The future for Navig8 Biz is bright.

We know we have something that is unexpected and comes from deep within our DNA.

Our mission is to increase the success rate, improve businesses' profitability, and create 6 Star businesses worldwide.

JOANNE BROOKS

Joanne Brooks' persona is down-to-earth, and her energy is contagious. She has spoken at many events, empowering and education women and business owners across the country. Jo is a leading specialist in the field of business education, having founded and built her own start-up from zero to 30m in only 18 months.

Among this, her personal story has been likened to a Hollywood screenplay – a story that must be told.

With a career spanning over 20 years in finance and banking, and a further 15 years in education, Joanne has also educated and mentored hundreds of clients in commercial lending, career development and business acumen.

Now the CEO of Navig8 Biz in partnership with Nick Barnsdall. Navig8Biz was born from a simple need: Business owners need support, experience, empathy, community, and guidance from those who had travelled the business road many times before. They needed to understand how to grow their business, and strategically map out those steps from start to finish.

You can reach Joanne via:

(W)   www.navig8biz.com

(E)   joanne@navig8biz.com

(M)   +61 434 602 024

CHAPTER SIX

YOU CAN'T DELIVER A 6 STAR SERVICE AND IMPROVE PEOPLE'S LIVES IF YOU'RE NOT PROFITABLE!

I set up **CINCH Transform** (formerly CINCH Finance Pty Limited) in 2014 to help purpose-driven businesses achieve more efficient outcomes and maximise limited funding. I do this using a ten-phase transformation program strengthening businesses to serve communities better, which improves people's lives and help more vulnerable people.

'**Profitability is a shallow goal if it doesn't have a real purpose, and the purpose has to be to share the profits with others.**'
Howard Schultz

No matter what market you operate in, your organisation needs to be profitable, to serve, sustain and invest in infrastructure, systems and people.

Why?

Because you can't have an impact if you're not profitable and profits provide the resources to continue achieving your purpose, which is also an element of a 6 Star business!

The organisation came to me because it believed getting a better understanding of its numbers would help reduce costs and lessen the impact of revenue changes across the Disability Sector. This understanding of what was required extended to calculating unit costs, identifying Key Performance Indicators (KPI's), calculating workforce capacity and running through an array of possible financial models to demonstrate what needed to change to make a profit.

As you might guess, this is all work related to the financial aspects of running an organisation. Yet, it's our people who are vital for improving profitability. So we needed to find a way to communicate this information to key stakeholders who weren't necessarily well-versed in finances or the complexities of running a business.

To operate successfully, we came up with a two-part plan:

1. Spend as much time as needed to understand the organisation's numbers to build a profitable yet sustainable financial model; and

2. Work with the organisation's people to change the culture, increase leadership performance which increases their impact in the community.

For three years, we worked with the organisation to improve its service delivery practices, focusing on leadership, communication and creating a "can do" culture. During that time, there were pricing changes in the market which presented even more challenges. However, the hard work paid off.

Today, we can say this organisation didn't have to wind up; our review resulted in quantified recommendations for a potential saving of 27.7% of revenue and an increase in efficiency, which allowed delivery of services to more people and the increase in revenue, straight to profit.

Two years later, we receive word they are operating profitably, reducing waitlists and looking to broaden their geographical reach (to serve more people).

Purpose and Profit

Originally coming from the commercial sector and in a new market, I quickly found out talking about "Profit" was quietly frowned upon in the not-for-profit sector. I agree the purpose of many successful businesses is not simply to make a profit. Howard Schultz, the long-standing chairperson and CEO of Starbucks, links profit to 'real purpose' as quoted at the start of this chapter. Customers thought me 'crazy' however quickly realised to deliver a 6 Star service; you needed to be profitable.

While I agree that profit is not the main priority, a 6 Star business requires profit to support impact, which is the purpose behind your organisation. After all, you can make a profit which directly impacts your ability to provide services; the more profit, the more services you can deliver, the more people you can serve and the greater impact you have. Time and again, we've found our most successful clients make a profit, which they then reinvest into the important work they do.

Why is Profitability Important in a 6 Star Business?

There are many aspects to profit, including how an organisation engages the community, stakeholders, the systems to operate efficiently, leadership, the quality of products and services, and its impact on customers. Here are seven critical areas to achieve profitability in a 6 Star business.

1. **Clarity** – understanding the organisation and its finances, the various levers key to improving performance. You need to know what makes the organisation 'tick', and the best way to do this is to talk to the people, customers, review systems and outputs. Discover what the most significant Key Performance Indicators are and how they can be measured. Pick the five to seven key financial and non-financial measures that matter and clarify how they all fit together.

2. **Scenario Modelling** – with this clarity, develop a range of financial models and assumptions which show the impact under different circumstances and be creative with what 6 Star would look like? Use KPI's as the basis for developing the scenarios and communicate with stakeholders, so they understand the potential impact and various decisions which impact profitability.

3. **Review and Recommendations** – scenario modelling is no good without clear and concise commentary, which help stakeholders determine the next steps and longer-term course of action.

4. **Low-Hanging Fruit** – look for the quick wins to achieve an initial Return on Investment (ROI) before investing more and more money into a change management process. A few quick wins will help align the team with outcomes and create momentum for further change.

5. **Workforce Capacity, Efficiency & Mindset** – staff utilisation (where, how and on which activity people spend their time) is one of the more significant levers that impact a service-based organisation's profitability. Understanding the workforce's capacity, skills, and efficiency will determine whether there are systems, cultural or efficiency gaps. All of which take time to improve.

6. **Report and Measure What Matters** – being accountable for our decisions is one of the hardest things to measure; however, it makes the difference between good and Six Star. Measure the more significant KPI's, report and analyse the changes each month to confirm the right decisions are being made, and performance is improving, including profits.

7. **Purpose** - communicating your purpose throughout the organisation is a 6 Star quality, differentiating between 'doing alright financially' and seriously being profitable. When the leadership team is clear on performance outcomes, they encourage respectful/candid feedback, which stimulates innovation, leading to greater profitability.

Turning things around

Make decisions. Don't sit on the fence and wait until you fall off!

If you make a decision and it doesn't work out, make another decision and change the outcome. Continuous Improvement is another critical factor in maintaining profitability. When increasing the success from short to long term sustainability, dedication is required from the key leadership team to staff on the frontline.

I worked with an organisation with the challenge of maintaining its core services for a low-profit margin product. Like the previous stories, the business was losing money, which threatened to strain resources. However, there was plenty of demand for services. I sat with the organisation's key stakeholders and ran through the most critical numbers and key drivers. We came up with a range of profitable financial models, discussed how the transformation would impact various business areas, developed a plan, put it in a language that the board and leadership team could understand, and presented it.

The organisation followed the recommendations and implemented several internal changes, consisting of quick wins and a longer-term investment plan resulting in a profit. They reinvested more money in people and infrastructure, which allowed for further cost savings and growth opportunities. As a result, the organisation had a road map to transform the group and operate profitably.

Since the transformation, the organisation has taken advantage of several growth opportunities and acquired several of the competition who weren't managing successfully.

Most importantly, they are helping more people, which was made possible by trading profitably!

Profitability is Better Serving Communities

Imagine waking up one morning to hear the organisation supporting you in everyday living activities for the last ten years gone into voluntary administration. You're not sure what that means; however, you can see the worry and stress in the face of your care worker when they turn up. Unfortunately, this has been the reality for organisations (large and small) that don't have the resources to continue. Profitability, however, removes this uncertainty and changes peoples' lives.

Winding up can sometimes be inevitable, though making great decisions, monitoring key performance indicators, increasing leadership performance, engaging customers and investing in systems and people reduces the risk of this happening.

Implementing change means very little if you do not measure performance. Measure what matters and regularly report to key stakeholders, which improves communication and creates further opportunities for your organisation and the people you serve.

An organisation helping over two hundred of our most vulnerable people, employing over one hundred staff and a waitlist of people looking for service, had given themselves eighteen months before they would look at winding up. Without profit, the organisation had no resources and could not continue delivering services. In addition, the organisation would leave a gap in the market, disrupting families and community if it ceased. Achieving profit was the key to turning this organisation around.

The change came from an early focus on understanding the numbers and improving the leadership team. As a result, the CEO has grown revenue by seven times its original turnover, employed three hundred and thirty-three more people and achieved a staggering 700% growth in four years. That's a remarkable turnaround given the fact the group was eighteen months away from closing. While there's still work to do in developing internal systems to support growth and sustain profitability, the organisation is well on its way to helping more people in need.

What a 6 Star impact!

I believe every organisation can be a 6 Star business, and transformation may be the key between a good business and a great business. When transformation happens fluidly, everybody inside the organisation aligns with the organisation's purpose.

Purpose creates clarity, which leads to profitability and serving more people.

ABOUT THE AUTHOR

DAVID HUBBARD, CEO, CINCH TRANSFORM

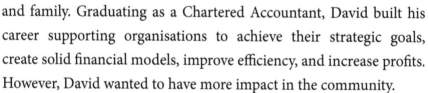

David Hubbard is an *Authentic, Considerate,* and *Diligent* person, as described by many clients, close friends, and family. Graduating as a Chartered Accountant, David built his career supporting organisations to achieve their strategic goals, create solid financial models, improve efficiency, and increase profits. However, David wanted to have more impact in the community.

David purposely drew upon the 20 years of commercial finance experience to strengthen purpose-driven businesses to serve more of the vulnerable and improve people's lives.

That's why CINCH Transform was founded in 2014.

Since then, David and his team have worked tirelessly with many Purpose-Driven Organisations to develop profitable business models, adapt to change and fulfilling their purpose of helping more

vulnerable people.

P.S. 'I can't change the direction of the wind, but I can adjust my sails to always reach my destination.' Jimmy Dean

Visit www.cinchtransform.com.au for further case studies, download the 10 Phase CINCH Transformation Program and find out more about why David does what he does.

CHAPTER SEVEN

BE A 6 STAR BUSINESS BY FINDING YOUR AUTHENTIC SELF-WORTH

When my father came home early, it was never a good sign. The air seemed to freeze every time he stepped into the flat. My sister, Mum and I had our guards up; we were on red alert. I always hoped I would not get caught for chores not done or not done well enough.

I hated him for his constant criticism of me. He brought home stress from his business, and his normal states were anger, blame, fear, and anxiety. Always ready to explode, he just needed a tiny spark. So although I knew I should love him, I failed and concluded that something was wrong with me and that I was not good enough for him to accept and love me as I am.

At the age of eight, my strategy became to prove myself worthy of love or to escape from home or both. I excelled in sports and was always looking for the external validation that I did not get at home. Thus, a wrong map was installed in my head: not good enough, unworthy of love, not deserving and more.

For thirty-five years, I've tried to resolve my self-worth issues in many ways, such as extensive travelling, then moving to three different countries, changing careers from corporate to sports, network marketing, trading and investing. I set up new businesses, tried spirituality to get away from it all, got married, and lost myself in books, seminars, and workshops as I studied the mind for more than fifteen years.

My baggage was heavy, and my family were sceptical about me ever changing. I had two jobs when I arrived home my home business started. At that time, my mantra was "work for paying the bills and home business to break out of it". But despite hard work, my business was not making money.

My family life and relationships with my kids were badly affected. I felt I was a loser, a total failure, even falling asleep at work. And I experienced my childhood patterns in everything I did.

Then my wife one day proposed divorce. It was the last straw.

Years ago, my mentor offered a profound answer to the question, "How come I am unable to help my eleven-year-old son with his lack of confidence?" (He could not score goals in games.)

He paused for a few seconds then asked a very powerful question that has put me on a different life path.

"Is his dad scoring goals in life?"

My eventual breakthroughs have come from working with a subconscious mind specialist who helped me separate from my old patterns and access the hidden corners of my mind to clear the junk. Since then, we have both scored goals.

What is self-worth? It is who you believe yourself to be, your relationship with yourself. It determines the quality of life in every respect. It is strongly connected to self-image, self-confidence, self-respect and self-love. I help with them all.

I find that most people carry patterns of self-sabotage for twenty to forty years. A few sessions with a reputable specialist like myself enable people to become aware and resolve their old patterns.

One of these transformations helped **Peter Daly-Dickson** conceive the 6 Star business podcast series that led to this book you are reading now. Peter has created space for creativity and contribution in place of the old limitations he had been carrying.

Are you repeating things in life or business? What are you avoiding?

Although it may look like it has nothing to do with your business success, that area could hold the most significant breakthrough in your business.

One of my clients presented her problem. She had been crossing paths with ignorant people at many facades of life: business, driving, and shopping. We found that she had subconsciously picked up judgment from her Mum. With my help, she has taken the labelling and judging filter off her eyes and released her anger. As a result, she has new experiences with people and found her compassionate self as she shares herself in a new way.

While she avoided situations with possible emotional triggers before, now she finds peace and acceptance instead. She created space for creativity and became inspired to expand her business and vision into an unorthodox online approach to beauty. She is guiding and supporting businesses during the changing and challenging environment of the new economy. These results are fascinating! It is just one of her breakthroughs.

Become a 6 Star Business Leader

You are the ultimate building block of your business. When you become a 6 Star leader, the rest will come automatically. So you'd better get rock solid now, before the pressure of bigger business tests you or crushes you.

Can you find the repeating recurring patterns in your business? In what way are they a reflection of you or your unresolved past?

Your business is a projection of your subconscious mind.

Are you willing to have a 6 Star mind driving your business?

Would you put a VW beetle engine into a Porsche?

You may not have worked out why implementing expensive strategies in your business did not work for you. Beware of signing up for new ones before you study yourself via this chapter. There are many programs that I call "strategies" or "how to" courses that talk about headspace or mindset, explaining how important it is.

But they spend little time barely scratching the surface and move on to teach people how and what to do, with processes and steps. I agree it is essential to do the right things. They work perfectly if your mind is aligned to the outcome. Until then, the war is on between subconscious needs and conscious goals, and battleground ground in your head. The subconscious takes over when you are under pressure. Taking your business to the next level will create pressure and a need for change, but your programming is always in the way of your jump to the next level. That is why you are where you are; it is congruent to your current inner wiring.

It is very easy to become a victim of your limiting programming. If I asked this swimming fish to explain to me what water is. What answer would I get?

What is mindset or subconscious programming?

These are the sums of your earlier decisions, experiences, adopted attitudes, values, negative emotions you hang onto (mostly unaware), voices in your head or stories you tell yourself. Meanings and associations to certain things, situations or people are stored in your mind. And your identity or personality is a collection of your earlier experiences.

This mind does anything to get love, connection, attention and food, feel accepted and find peace. These are your main drivers. Thrown out of the tribe/family or rejection means literally starvation or death. Adopting twisted behaviour is a solution like disconnecting from emotions, being angry, sad, getting sick or being shy.

A Business Never Outperforms the Psychology of the Leader.

If you are carrying patterns of "Not good enough," "I don't deserve it," "Unworthy," "I haven't got time," "I haven't got money," "I don't know the right people," or similar, you just keep repeating the old results. Your mind will make these beliefs your reality.

Are you ready to get back into the driver seat of your mind?

Are you sure you want to keep telling yourself disempowering stories? They become real.

I tell my clients often that I have maximum respect for you but no respect for your stories.

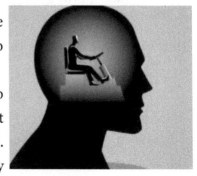

Happiness is not important to the subconscious mind, nor does it care what you have set out as a goal. Evolution has equipped you to stay alive and procreate. Your emotional patterns and limitations drive your focus, attention and your results.

I have become a master at talking to the survival mind to discover and change the programming. I help you remove your limitations. The result is inner peace, self-compassion and alignment towards creating what you want. Your creativity starts to flow.

This formula brought to life the **"Peace with money" home study course** after a fantastic transformation of a client. She has struggled for forty years with sadness, fears and multiple limiting beliefs. Finally, she is back in the driver's seat, and she is empowered to change money reality for the masses.

Your 6 Star leader transformation steps:

> ***Commitment**
>
> ***Clarity**
>
> ***Release & Realign**
>
> ***Focus, Self-worth – Self-image**
>
> ***Develop influence & inspiring community**
>
> ***Action & productivity**

Your business is teaching you about yourself.

Are you open to being taught?

Are you attracting employees and clients with your unresolved childhood events?

The idea of doing it alone is gone. Instead, winning teams are the key to success.

Do you have a reputation for producing outstanding results?

Are you working towards it if you don't?

I love Aveline and Peter bringing 6 Star business consciousness into the world. I am behind them with all my experience and knowledge.

Your ingredients to become a 6 Star business success:

*Short how-to education

*Networking up

*Mastermind

*Rituals

*Quarterly recharge min 3-4 days

* 1/1 reputable mindset coach (must produce a change in your life) + industry mentor

Which one are you not doing?

I have written so much more to help you transform. You can have my original uncut version. Email me at my.rct.coach@gmail. com

People regularly see me and tell me they had serious challenges behind them, and now they are ok. I hear: "I have got this under control," even from the 6 Star community. They say, "I have been working on healing this for decades". I ask five questions; the emotional baggage is ripped open, they are back in the past, physiology shifts, tears start to flow, etc. This indicates that it has not been resolved. It has been festering under the surface and affects every decision they make in the present and future.

Is it clear the psychology of a leader of $150K and $50 Mil business is remarkably different? There is a process in between.

There is a 6 Star version of you inviting you from the future to play a bigger game.

Accept the invitation and buckle up!

ENDRE HOFFMANN

Endre helps people to restore 6 Star self-worth and move rapidly toward goals. First, he finds the root of negative emotions and limiting patterns with accuracy. Then he does instant surgery to facilitate fast & lasting transformations. Endre creates such a safe space where his clients drop old paradigms and experience life from a new identity that they started to call him the Doctor of Self-Worth.

He reconnects his clients to their original 6 Star version experiencing peace, joy, fun & contribution. According to the Doctor, the real pandemic is various large-scale mind viruses that have infected business leaders who unconsciously sabotage their own and their employees' progress.

Are you ready to take the red pill and taste your 6 Star version?

Reach out to book your diagnostic appointment now! https://calendly.com/doctor-of-self-worth/self-worth-diagnosis

You can reach Endre via:

https://www.facebook.com/Doctor.of.Self.Worth/

https://www.linkedin.com/in/Doctor-of-Self-Worth

and other social media platforms

M: +61 434 760 903

CHAPTER EIGHT

"The things to do are the things that need doing, that you see need to be done and that no one else seems to see need to be done".
Buckminster Fuller

In 1992 I stood on a 3000-acre property in subtropical NSW, Australia. Since my career began, I imagined an education business designed to transform lives. My preferred tool was adventure-based learning - outdoors.

Learning and growth using carefully managed risk-taking and adventure expose young adults to phenomenal learning opportunities. Simultaneously it makes an educator vulnerable to litigation. Being responsible for thousands of souls in the outdoors each year is fraught. Extreme weather, student misbehaviour, equipment failure, and occasional ambulance visits create massive pressure for small business owners.

After twenty years of impacting the growth and development of future generations, the huge responsibility overtook me, and I sold the business.

The purchaser, a large '5 Star' not for profit, continued to deliver exceptional educational outcomes, world-class staff training, state of the art equipment and complex safety protocols. BUT, they forgot how crucial customer experience is to thrive.

Raising prices exponentially, changing protocols and administration processes overnight, miscommunicating business model changes, and making clients' lives more complex delivered the message, 'we don't care'. Nine years later, my baby finally perished.

Activated by that experience, I realised I often feel bored, invisible or disconnected as a consumer. So I set out to help businesses connect and appreciate.

6 Star businesses don't simply provide 'stuff'. They also do the emotional labour that leverages the human spirit to generate sincere connection. This transforms relationships and lives.

The magic of sensational customer experience may leverage wealth. Careful thought and a good intention are simple. However, delivering consistent, delightful, engaging experiences that maximise lifetime customer value is not easy; it requires emotional labour.

In 2019 a hundred billion dollars was spent on digital marketing internationally - two hundred and fifty billion in 2020 and over half a trillion dollars in 2021.

How can our message be heard when the digital noise is forever amplifying? It seems only those companies with the most money can avoid being left-swiped and deleted.

We're hyper-connected, and yet collectively, we've never felt more distant, inadequate and alone. Our essence, who we are, has become lost in the commercialisation of our identity.

Humanising business is vital now!

In marketing and sales, B2B, B2C and B2G are common abbreviations. These B2X shortcuts are BS. Human to human (H2H) is the only focus that makes any sense.

When did you last experience a robot ordering a burger, an algorithm purchasing a coaching program or a laptop calling an electrician? Purchasing is still a uniquely human phenomenon.

Even the most analytical of us make buying decisions emotionally then justify rationally. How we make our customers feel is what makes us remarkable, memorable and preferred.

Finding authentic ways to attract and keep genuine attention is crucial.

Great customer service is invisible because it's expected.

Imagine you and your partner having a meal at a local restaurant. You expect a piping hot meal in a reasonable time, made with quality ingredients. You assume your preferences will be noted and your food served with a smile in a clean establishment where the ambience, décor and price match your expectations.

All these things are entry-level requirements for a successful restaurant.

We are seeking a memorable experience where we are recognised, remembered, acknowledged, engaged, and empathised with in a way that creates 'WOW!' We know we must return.

Five Steps to Being a 6 Star Business

1. Empathise

"Could a greater Miracle Take Place than for us to look through each other's eyes for an instant"
Henry David Thoreau

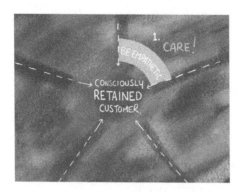

Empathy requires us to listen, observe, intuit and see the world from our customer's perspective first, from the outside in.

If we don't care then, our customers never will. Our challenges are of zero interest to clients. They want their problems solved with careful and deliberate intent.

Caring isn't about being a bleeding heart or a soft touch, nor is it fleeting or manipulative – it's about being human and connected. To maximise lifetime customer value, create a connection and a belief in each other, like a long-term healthy marriage. As consumers, we spend much of our time feeling we are being handled, processed and transacted.

Take the aviation sector.

Since 1987 the Airbus A320, with nearly 10,000 in service, has become a common sight.

Flying in an A320 with a budget airline, we are labelled 'passengers' and safely and efficiently processed. However, it feels entirely different when a full-service airline calls us 'guests' on their A320, provides hot towels as we are seated and deliver warm service and free cold beer.

When the machinery is the same, the experience is what differentiates.

Our DNA hard-wires us to seek recognition, thoughtfulness, appreciation and acknowledgement. Your competition lurks with a kind gesture, smile, insightful questions, thank you and meaningful connection. They are already calling back, keeping track, remembering names and numbers, caring, keeping promises and anticipating your customers/their prospects needs.

Caring is profitable, so how do your customers know they matter?

2.   Ubuntu & the Gratitude Economy

"Our first step to becoming the one our customers choose is to be the one who chooses to see the customer."
Bernadette Jiwa

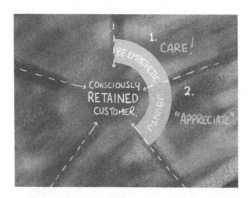

If empathy is about looking 'outside-in', then Ubuntu is about our attitude - from the inside-out.

Ubuntu is a South African word that means 'I see and honour you. I recognise you. I am more because you are in my world.' The energy behind the word expresses, 'Let's leverage our collective genius to create the synergy that will solve your problem or help you realise your opportunity'.

It's an expression of appreciation. 'Your decision to purchase from me is the fuel I need to have the impact I seek to make'.

Mary, our local barista, recently demonstrated Ubuntu in action Mary is always chatty with a knack for remembering our coffee order preferences.

I noticed her using sign language to communicate with a customer, so I asked if someone in her family was deaf.

'Oh, no', she smiled. 'That's John. He's a regular, and he's deaf. For ages, I've wanted him to have the same experience as everyone else here, so I taught myself some AUSLAN (sign language) and really surprised him.' John's face showed he clearly felt special to be included.

How do you and your team 'see' and honour your stakeholders?

3. Delight. Create 'Wow'.

Don't just satisfy your customers. Delight them. Anyone who has happy customers is likely to have a pretty good future.
Warren Buffet

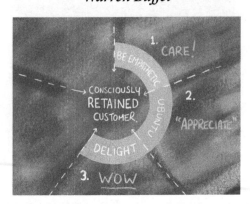

Ask any Disney employee what their role is. Invariably the answer is, 'To make people happy'.

Disney cast members (staff) are committed to delighting at every touchpoint. Creating extraordinary moments of 'WOW' is the company's lifeblood.

Being magical requires consistent effort, training and discipline. The Disney rule is, 'When you are on stage (at work), delight every person with whom you interact'.

Any business can create delight.

Mike and I are high schoolmates. He is now an executive of a major Australian university.

On a pre-Covid, multi-stop, world university lecture tour, Mike endured a forgettable 72-hour period.

He woke one morning in Spain, unable to move due to a mystery back injury.

He was medi-evacuated to a hospital in London for a barrage of tests. Then, just as the powerful pain medication took effect, his phone rang to say that his mum had passed away in Australia.

He transferred to a nearby hotel, grief-ridden, to figure out the logistics of flying home.

In his rush, Mike spilt a glass of orange juice onto his computer keyboard. In that moment, his frustration and grief got the better of him, and he broke down.

The knock at the door indicated the arrival of room service. The waiter saw Mike's desk and what had happened.

Soon after, there was another knock at the door. There the waiter stood, beaming, with a brand-new keyboard in hand. He gave it to Mike and left. A random act of 'wow'.

Someone had truly cared! Any guesses where he stays in London now?

How do you 'Disneyfy' your business?

4.   **Create Experiences. Be memorable.**

'The only purpose of customer experience
is to change feelings'. Seth Godin

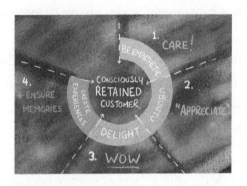

It turns out that it's not the experiences we have but the memory of those experiences that become the key factor in our purchasing decisions.

In his 2010 TED Talk, Behavioural Economist Daniel Kahneman, winner of the 2002 Nobel Memorial Prize in Economic Sciences, explains that there are about six hundred million moments in an average life, a moment being three seconds. So, there are about six million moments per month and most of them are ignored by our 'remembering self'.

What makes an experience memorable are beginnings, changes, significant moments, and endings. Thus, endings are critically important and, in many cases, endings dominate.

Businesses need to ensure they create an avalanche of brain-chemical pathways, especially at the first touchpoint, peak experience, and endpoint with a client. If we wish to maximise the lifetime value of our client, our role is to ensure not only the quality of our product but also the actual memory creating moments.

Providing experiences that etch us into our customer's memories with an injection of feel-good brain chemicals is astonishingly simple, but it requires forethought and work.

Once perfected and delivered systematically, high-quality customer experiences become rocket fuel for business growth that offers powerful protection from competitors and economic downturns.

What experiences do you provide to ensure appreciative customers?

5. **Loyalty Begets Loyalty**

'Extreme Loyalty is gained by over-delivering on exaggerated expectations'. Darrell Hardidge.

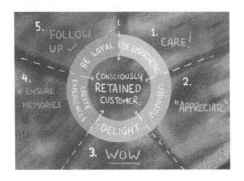

True loyalty is relational, not transactional or driven by a power differential. Instead, it's generated by countless purposeful whispers that lead to predictable and repeatable attitudes, feelings and long-term positive outcomes. Loyalty is not generated by customer service departments or so-called 'loyalty cards'.

Loyalty is fuelled by the memory of promises kept. It's not about watertight contracts, legalese, nepotism or manipulation. It's anchored in our preparedness to take 100% responsibility for being good to our word, no matter what.

When customers appreciate what you do for them with predictability and surprise, they continue to choose you. They'll remember how you made them feel in preference to what you did.

Loyalty is especially built during times of crisis. So, close the loop and reconcile when times are tough or mistakes are made. 6 Star businesses act on the golden rule. 'Do Unto Others'.

What's your loyalty' bounce back' plan for when the wheels fall off?

Exceptional customer service is the minimum benchmark.

Empathy, appreciation, delight and remarkable memories drive fierce loyalty. 6 Star businesses are unrelenting in their pursuit of loyalty and authentic, WOW experiences.

That's the 'Now What'.

GREG SMITH, CEO- Send Handwritten

Having founded his first business in 1992, Greg Smith is a veteran of the experiential (outdoor) education industry. While their peers endured sedentary, test-driven, result-focused school curricula, Greg's young adult clients expeditioned outdoors. The natural world was a vehicle to help answer three enduring questions. Who am I? Who are we? What is the difference we seek to make?

Having sold that business with his wife, Greg founded Swim For Your Life and Specialised Aquatic Therapy to transform the lives of children with a disability.

Greg's current project, Send Handwritten, is a marketing experience company intent on helping clients secure meetings with difficult to reach decision-makers. When the marketing norm went digital, Send Handwritten went analogue (with an intriguing modern twist) to capture attention with authentically handwritten, exquisitely designed, and personalised wax-sealed mail.

Greg remains inspired to help others have the impact they seek to make.

You can reach Greg via:

greg@sendhandwritten.com.au

www.sendhandwritten.com.au

0429872386

https://www.linkedin.com/in/greg-smith-87533a11/

https://calendly.com/sendhandwritten1?month=2021-04

CHAPTER NINE

TECHNOLOGICAL INNOVATION AND ITS IMPACT ON BUSINESS PROFITABILITY

Leaving behind an impact is one of the most significant contributions a business owner can make in this world. The dictionary definition of impact is "a powerful effect that something, especially something new, has on a situation or person." In today's context, technology easily qualifies as that 'something new.' Without a doubt, incorporating AI and machine learning in your business processes can dramatically impact your customers and their journey.

Throughout history, humanity has looked for ways to make life easier. First came the wheel, then the car, laptops followed desktop computers, and now our smartphones are improving on the telephone. Over the years, our need to be more efficient, save time and improve productivity has been a driving force behind significant societal changes.

There's a famous quote by Peter Drucker that says, "Quality in a service or product is not what you put into it; it is what the customer gets out of it." Saving customers' time and getting the job done is the greatest motivation for businesses to use technology to improve the customer journey and experience. Tech can save the customer time and deliver the product or service faster than one's competitors. If a company knows what a customer wants and delivers on those needs quickly and efficiently before anyone else, who do you think the customers will choose?

I've believed in this ideology since the very start of my professional life. "Invest in Technology" is the advice one of my first bosses gave me. This is about providing the customer with tools and a competitive advantage to deliver at a high quality and faster rate than before.

For example, one of the most difficult challenges any new entrepreneur faces is to take the first step. There's nothing more susceptible to procrastination than a blank page. A ready way to make an impact is to make it easy for your customers to take that first step.

When I started YourNameFree.com, we provided online tools to simplify the internet domain name registration process. Our competitors had a multi-step procedure that required a waiting period. In addition, they demanded the customer learn the technical steps like defining a set of name servers for their domain name to resolve.

We created an impact by removing the obstacles, simplifying the forms, and putting in our name servers so that when the person's domain name was registered, they'd see a webpage with a set of instructions on what to do next. It was quick, intuitive, and straightforward.

What can you do to make life fast and easy for your customers? The answer to that question is how you can make an impact in their lives.

We followed this mantra at Resume.com, where we used technology to help young people build a captivating resume from scratch--one that gets them in the door. Over four million resumes were created using our intuitive flow. As a result, high-school students could get a better job than they would have had we not existed. And rather than charging everyone a fee (like our competitors were doing), we took the freemium model route, where a tiny percentage of working professionals paid a membership fee. The impact on people who never paid us a penny is a lasting reward.

Don't reserve impact strictly to paying customers. Your business can have an effect beyond those who open their wallet to you. As a 6 Star business, you want to leave every person you interact with in a better state than when they met you.

Even in a relatively non-technical business of holding a conference, technology can help you create an impact. For example, NamesCon was created as an internet domain name conference where the two major competitors had very different approaches. One held a conference for free, usually in exotic locations. The other charged a hefty registration fee which kept attendance low, but excellent food was served throughout the event.

We knew that to be successful, NamesCon needed a critical mass of attendees. So we used the technology in Facebook's advertising tools to target our prospective audience and notify them whenever someone they knew registered for our conference. We made it look like everyone was thinking about going until everyone was going! As a result, our first conference saw over six hundred attendees, and in three years, grew to over fifteen hundred attendees. The new owners of NamesCon continue to leverage technology to ensure that the conference is held online between in-person gatherings.

As for the impact, it was two-fold: the conference raised over half a million dollars for the WaterSchool.com charity and became the largest domain name conference in the world, where the testimonials were overflowing with thanks and appreciation. Thus, the impact was in actual lives saved and many lives affected.

The lesson here is not to get fixated on dollars and profit when building a 6 Star business. Instead, create a real impact in your customers' lives, and they will reciprocate their appreciation. Money is a 'thank you' for delivering value and impact.

Another example of creating impact is our current project, LOGO.com, using AI to help new businesses and individuals create a professional logo in less than 30 minutes. At first glance, this can have you scratching your head as to any real impact. But let's take a look at what we are using technology to replace here.

A business owner looking for a logo can expect to take 2 to 3 weeks to design their logo through an agency, freelance designer, or logo contest. If someone wants to turn their side gig into a business, they might build a website or order business cards. When they get to the step where they need to insert their logo, they tend to put their current task on hold while they go off to get their logo designed. If it takes too long, there is a strong possibility that the entire process gets derailed.

So, allowing customers to create a logo that they can use right away and get right back into ordering their set of business cards or building their website isn't just a small step; it's an integral part of starting their new business or perhaps their new life as an entrepreneur.

With our use of technology to create and deliver a logo almost instantly, the impact on the customer's life can be massive. Essentially, we are enabling our customers to launch their business idea in a weekend. So always look at what impact your product has on the customer that goes beyond the final sale. How it helps them save time and money, act faster or improve their station in life.

The Union of Sound Technology and the Customer's Journey.

When designed properly, technology can make the process of getting something done fun. Machines and computer programming can make it easier for you to do more in a lot less time and without the drudgery. The advances in computing power also mean that you can do some of the most complicated, creative tasks seemingly instantly, improving your customer impact.

Today, experience is everything, and a growing percentage of this experience is digital. Good technology gives customers the tools and ideas they need to execute something quickly and efficiently; the overall design and customer journey are more personal despite, or because of, a machine or a program powering it.

When it comes to building a business, customer experience can make or break the deal. This simple complexity is why artificial intelligence (AI) offers such an enormous value to businesses. For example, when we built our logo editor for LOGO.com utilising AI as a cornerstone, we spent the first few years researching all kinds of logo designs and analysing the conversations graphic designers would have with their customers. This ensured we would create something functional and valuable to the end customer. Graphic designers and design agencies cannot understand your exact vision without numerous conversations, and they cannot be expected to churn out hundreds of logos in a week. With AI, we're able to do both in seconds!

Customers aren't just getting logo design ideas; they also get the opportunity to build on those ideas using the logo editor. Putting formerly complex tools directly into the hands of our customers, they can change the colours, play around with the layouts, explore a vast library of icons and fonts, and edit the design to make it their own. Now, many of our customer reviews describe the process of logo designing as "fun"!

Giving the user a strong base and necessary tools gives them the power to do something they would have otherwise thought impossible without a professional and hours of back and forth for days or weeks.

Our logo designs are on par with those of professional human designers. We give customers options to get inspired and build their designs themselves for an incredibly low cost, but more importantly, quickly. From the moment they enter the website until they checkout, the whole journey usually takes less than twenty minutes.

When building this technology, we weren't just focused on the customer journey from the moment they enter the website to when they check out. That is just one aspect of the impact we are looking to achieve. Like all my other ventures, with LOGO.com, we wanted to go beyond the final sale. We understood that a good logo is just the beginning; new businesses need an entire branding package to get started. So, we gave them a website builder, a social media kit, and a complete branding suite that includes stock photos, brand guidelines, a free domain name, and more. We have the toolset to deliver an impact that will save the customer countless hours beyond their initial logo design.

Customer Experience is Directly Proportional to Profitability.

Because the customer can do more in less time, embracing technology makes the customer journey seamless and helps build a profitable business. For businesses looking to leverage technology and automation, the key is to identify areas that could use technology to save time. What can you build that can make a customer's life a little bit easier?

"Customer is king," and when you make them feel like one by saving them time, they will thank you by opening their wallet. Your competitors could be huge in comparison to you, but if you're able to create an impact in your customers' lives, even with something as simple as a logo, you'll build a successful business.

RICHARD LAU, Founder LOGO.com

Named 2004 "Domainer of the Year", Richard has generated millions of dollars in revenue in the domain industry.

NamesCon began as an idea in the fall of 2012 and is now part of the Godaddy family. Another recent exit (to Indeed.com), Resume.com aids millions of job seekers to build their resumes online and provides a home for their online CV for life.

His newest project is LOGO.com, an AI-powered logo maker that offers a complete branding suite.

You can reach Richard via:

Web: www.logo.com

LinkedIn: https://www.linkedin.com/in/richardlau/

CHAPTER TEN

HOW TO SUCCEED WITH HUMANITY IN BUSINESS, BY LISTENING

(Whilst turning your clients into advocates!)

I was in a fog of fear, my mind in a state of terror. I tried to distract myself with what I could see. The sun was shining, and I noticed the leaves were showing off vibrant red and gold colours. It was cold as we drove to the hospital. I was hoping that I was paranoid and over-protective of our soon to be first-born baby.

It was November 2001. I was 26 weeks pregnant and had just announced on social media that I was having a baby. I was in the third trimester - it felt safe to do so.

We arrived at the hospital; my heart was pounding, I was trying not to panic. We saw a midwife, and then fifteen minutes later, a doctor appeared in front of me with a grave expression. "I'm so sorry," he began. These were the three words I dreaded the most.

Our son, James, had died. I couldn't breathe. I couldn't believe it. I wouldn't believe it. But I had no choice.

Losing James was the hardest thing I've ever endured. But he taught me so much about life, the importance of empathy, care, love and how listening is such an essential part of everything. He taught me to be strong, to keep focused and determined, which gave me hope for the future.

Ten years on, and I'm building my business as a legacy to my boys (yes, I was lucky enough to have two more beautiful boys). This chapter is in part for James, who taught me the value of humanity in a harsh world. It is for my 9-year-old son and all the children who are our future – who need to know the importance of embracing humanity in life *and* business.

It is also for my 7-year-old son, who said recently, "When I grow up, I want to work with you to make the world a better place."

So, with the hope that we *can* make "the world a better place", - my vision is to bring humanity back into the world of business.

I'd like to think that the work I do today will impact the next generation and that alongside technology which is moving so fast, we embrace humanity in business and all that it brings with it, from laughter, love and kindness to the ability to listen. To me, all of these ingredients are the key to achieving a 6 Star business.

What Listening Can Do for Your Business

I believe the art of listening is one of the most important human skills we have; it's at the heart of our humanity, and that it is often lost in business. If we focus on listening to the people we work with; we can only improve.

Ultimately, people are the most important part of any business. Of course, you and your team are the core of your business and good communication and listening is critical. But it's essential to nurture your relationship with your clients; without your clients you don't have a business.

How can you increase your client engagement, client loyalty and encourage your clients to be your advocates? The first step is to take the time to listen. By listening, you can learn what your clients' greatest needs are so that you can serve them better. After all, doesn't everyone like to be heard?

Think about how you relate and engage with your friends. Part of the reason you are friends is that you care, you listen to their problems (and they listen to yours), you laugh together, you talk and share. Together you are better. You bring more humanity into the relationship.

Why not bring elements of this into your relationship with your clients? By listening and being more human, you will show you genuinely care and want to help them more, which will develop their trust and loyalty towards you; and who knows, your relationship with your clients could turn into a friendship. I know it has for me with several clients over the years.

As a start, you should aim for a partnership-led relationship as opposed to a transactional relationship. With this kind of thinking, everyone wants to succeed together, whatever it takes.

It's worth remembering; it's far more cost-effective to keep your clients happy than to get new clients. According to Amy Gallo of the Harvard Business Review, *"acquiring a new customer is anywhere from five to twenty-five times more expensive than retaining an existing one."*

Therefore, it's critical for all businesses to look at how to keep their clients happy and engaged and to convert them into advocates. The best way to ensure client advocacy is to be more human by engaging more with your clients. Reach out to them, listen to them, hear what they want and seek to understand what they value so you can serve them better.

I interview the customers/clients of my clients to find out what is working well and perhaps not so well. By being an impartial 'listener', their clients can give honest feedback about their supplier and offer suggestions for improvements, which is so much more in-depth and intuitive than an online form can ever be.

Once I've spoken and listened to a selection of clients, I then give feedback and recommendations, enabling my clients to improve and better engage with their clients.

I have been compared to a marriage counsellor for business as I am an independent listener, able to uncover golden nuggets and insights from clients that have led to businesses improving and growing. The intelligence gathered from interviewing clients has had a powerful impact on their business, enabling them to:

1. Improve communications and conversations with clients, developing trust and loyalty
2. Identify at-risk clients and develop plans to improve relationships with them
3. Develop new services and products
4. Build credibility with investors
5. Increase the pipeline (new and existing business) and grow revenue!

Interviewing and listening to clients leads to a better business and servicing an increasing number of client advocates with care and humanity.

Here's an example of how powerful listening to your clients can be. One business I worked with, which serves some of the biggest brands globally, was rapidly losing clients because they were over-promising and under-delivering, resulting in a lack of client trust. One of their clients said the way they were being treated left her feeling 'bereft'.

However, by taking the time to listen to her and their other clients, taking their suggestions for improvement, and being accountable to their clients, I helped them turn their average customer satisfaction score from 22% to 74% in just four months. This built trust with their clients, saved relationships worth millions, enabled improved services and processes; whilst boosting the company's reputation.

How to Turn Clients into Advocates

From the many interviews I've undertaken with clients, here are three activities I recommend people do more of within their business:

1. **Develop better communications with clients.** Be intentional in all your communications. Look at how you are engaging with them – from insights and events to digital and human interaction. Is there any part of this engagement that you can improve?

2. **Put a client advocacy process into place.** Once you have identified the most common contact you have with your clients, review them and make sure you have regular and improved engagement beyond standard newsletters and social media interaction. Ensure you are reaching out to them at different stages of their life cycle with something of value to

give them what they need or want continually.

3. **Ask for feedback from your clients**. See what is working or not working, what they want and how you can improve. Ideally, have someone outside your organisation interview them, so the clients feel they can be open and honest in their feedback. Try to do this at least yearly and follow up with them to tell them what changes you may have made as a result of their feedback. **Be accountable to your clients.**

To note:

When I do this, I interview a selection of clients at different stages of their relationship with the business and those with varying satisfaction levels to find out the patterns that may emerge and pull together ideas for development and improvement for the business. Although most of the insight is qualitative, I add a quantitative element to the feedback, making it easier to compare future results and see the most significant issues.

And a little, but important, bonus - When interviewing my clients' clients over the years, they have complained about three things the most. These are:

i. lack of communication
ii. lack of processes
iii. lack of proactivity

I recommend every business focuses on improving these three areas. This alone could make massive improvements in business and client relationships.

I believe that if an organisation proactively looks at bringing more humanity into their business between team members and clients, instead of relying on technology, whilst considering how they can turn their clients into advocates, they can only do better and improve overall!

Summary

When I think back over the last ten years, I know that one of the things that kept me going was being listened to, heard, cared for, and loved. The power of listening and genuine human connection is vital in every part of our lives, especially in business. If we all proactively try to listen, care, laugh and communicate with honesty, and ultimately be more human, we can make the world a happier place.

When I think about the legacy I want to leave my children – it's a world where people communicate with humanity at the heart of all they do.

I look to the next ten years with excitement and hope, that together we can bring more humanity into business for all *three* of my boys and the rest of the world. And perhaps at least one of my sons will be working alongside me *"to make the world a better place,"* where we are all striving to give our clients a 6 Star experience by being more human!

REMENY ARMITAGE,
Founder of Brilliant & Human

Remeny is focused on bringing humanity back into business. She has over twenty years of experience working for various businesses in client advocacy and insight research, marketing and new business. Ultimately, she helps businesses understand what their clients REALLY think about them with the goal of turning their clients into advocates. In addition, her experience has helped build relationships between businesses and their clients in a human-centric way. She gets under the skin of a business by interviewing their clients and feeding back ways they can improve the business and engage with their clients in a human way. She has built up a range of methods that ensure business improvement and growth while building long-lasting relationships based on a solid foundation of trust and respect between businesses and their clients to turn them into advocates.

You can reach Remeny via:

(E)   remeny@brilliantandhuman.com

(L)   https://www.linkedin.com/in/remeny

(W)   www.brilliantandhuman.com

CHAPTER ELEVEN

EMBRACING LOVE IN BUSINESS

In June 2016, I was alone, relaxing in my flat, when I felt that something was just not quite right. I had a strange tingling and weakness in my right side, which was quickly getting worse.

Alarmed, I just managed to call 999 and thank goodness I did because, by the time I made it to hospital, I'd completely lost the use of my right arm and leg.

The medics at the hospital were brilliant but baffled. Their worst-case scenario was that it was an aneurism – potentially fatal. The following ten days were tough, waiting for a diagnosis. I've never felt so vulnerable or helpless.

Having one test after another to discount all sorts of syndromes, each sounding more ominous than the next, lying in my hospital bed partially paralysed, having lost my independence in a matter of hours, gives you a very different perspective.

With my health and mobility suddenly taken away, I thought of all the things I hadn't done with my life, my ambitions that were still unfulfilled.

I'd been in the business world for 40 years, building and running my own businesses and supporting many others. I love what I do, and my work is an intrinsic part of me - championing others, introducing like-minded people and connecting people who can help and support each other's endeavours. However, I was working with only a handful of entrepreneurs a year, travelling to meet my clients and offering tailor-made services to each one. Suddenly, that was all hanging by a thread, and I had to ask myself some tough, 'get real' questions.

My thoughts were full of 'what ifs'. What if I could never work again? What would I do? A key, practical question was, what if I couldn't travel anymore? I was currently wheelchair-bound, and I had to face the possibility that that may never change. Yet, I couldn't imagine not continuing to share my decades of business experience to support small business owners in improving their businesses and achieving their goals.

I thought about how I could overcome potential travel issues and change the logistics of how I worked. Instead of focusing my time on a small number of individuals in a face-to-face environment, I could inspire hundreds, maybe even thousands of entrepreneurs simultaneously, by making the most of all the virtual options now available to us.

Coming up with solutions to these 'what ifs' gave me a new sense of purpose during this scary time, a reason to keep going. I made myself a promise - if I survived, I was going to go for it.

Over the next year, with a lot of hard work, bloody-mindedness and support, I made slow progress, recovering from what turned out to be a rare form of stroke. First to crutches, then to a walking stick, then finally relearning to walk around unassisted. I had to learn to write all over again, to do up buttons. The list went on. Together with the fantastic support of family and friends, what drove me to keep going through all those trials and challenges was my new sense of purpose to help as many entrepreneurs as possible.

I now view that horrendous experience as a stroke of luck, for which I will be eternally grateful. It has changed my life and the way I do business for the better. I've spent the last five years making good on that promise to myself to go for it, facing my fears and moving into uncharted territory. A website, public speaking, webinars, podcasts, articles, even a radio show. All to share my stories, my experience and my love for business as widely as possible. It fills me with a great deal of satisfaction to know that I've already helped hundreds more entrepreneurs than I would have before, to build their own 6 Star Businesses.

The time I spent recovering from my stroke accelerated the journey I was already on regarding the shift in how I wanted to do business. We've all heard the saying, "No-one's dying words are I wish I'd spent more time in the office." I'm sure that's true but, seeing as we inevitably must spend so much time working, as money trees are sadly only a fantasy, isn't it a gift to ourselves and everyone around us to be as content and energised as we can be? I don't just mean professionally. How many people do we observe, or maybe we only need to look in the mirror, feeling miserable when they get home? Preoccupied, dejected, unable to fully relax and enjoy their personal lives, which has a huge negative impact on their relationships with family and friends.

This resonates personally with me. For the first 25 years of my career, I was incredibly single-minded, motivated almost exclusively by financial goals. Looking back, I feel embarrassed at how

I did business, how my ambition and the decisions I made to make more money dominated the way I built businesses. Moreover, I was unaware of my behaviour's impact on others, uncaring about those around me. As a result, I invested little in my business relationships and ended up in toxic 'dog eat dog' environments.

Finally, things imploded in a perfect storm of bad experiences, and I'd had enough. I stepped back from the rat race and took some time out, knowing that something had to change. Around then, I read *The Five Dysfunctions of a Team* by Patrick Lencioni. It had a massive impact on me. It's written in story form, which beautifully and clearly illustrates the pitfalls of teams not working well together and demonstrating excellent team dynamics. I can't recommend it enough.

Gradually and organically, my natural leanings towards a more loving way of doing business came to the fore. Having been neglected and suppressed by the louder voice of one-dimensional, figures-oriented commercial practice, my passion and purpose grew and blossomed into the ethos and philosophy I champion today.

Yes, of course, every business needs to make money; otherwise, why bother? But I can guarantee, from personal experience, that running a business with the single, results-driven priority of making as much money as possible can be a stressful, uncomfortable and hollow experience. On the other hand, you *can* run a successful business from the heart, with the triple bottom line 'People. Planet. Profit.' always front of mind[1].

I often think of Warren Buffett, the CEO of Berkshire Hathaway, the famous American investment company with billions of dollars of assets under management. As a 'traditional, corporate white male' in his 90s, you wouldn't necessarily expect to hear him use 'love' when he describes successful business practice. Yet, that's precisely what he does. When asked about the secret of his success, he says that after their teams do all their analysis and pore over the numbers of a potential investee, Buffett insists on personally meeting the CEO. He looks them in the eye and tries to work out whether they love money or love the business. Berkshire Hathaway only invests when the CEO loves the business.

So, what does it mean to 'love business'? Love is a word that people often resist when it comes to business, feeling it's 'lovey dovey' and 'woo woo' and not appropriate or relevant in a business environment. I strongly disagree. When I think of love in business, I think of passion and purpose. Defining and articulating your purpose gives you the tools to build your business's DNA; think of it as Purpose + Values = 'DNA', or, if you prefer, the Culture of your business.

Running through your business like a stick of rock, the benefits of building and actively managing your business's DNA include attracting, recruiting and retaining better talent; improving productivity through a happier, more engaged team; boosting your P&L and increasing shareholder value[2]. This is an example of how advocating love in business has commercial benefits and creates and maintains a happy team. They're not mutually exclusive.

I must stress that this isn't a one-off exercise. There's no point doing this DNA work without constantly investing in and managing the DNA of your business. A couple of tips are (1) include values-based questions in your interviewing process and (2) incorporate measurable values-based behaviours in review meetings with each employee.

'Love in business' are three words that easily trip off the tongue, but it's essential to examine and implement the practical application behind the words. It's about *engagement* - what is your approach to running your business? How do you engage with your colleagues, your team, your suppliers, and your clients? Do you *acknowledge* your colleagues, clients or suppliers when they do a good job? And don't forget yourself! Are you *open*, genuine and transparent in the way that you deal with people? What about a spirit of *partnership* in your approach to business?

Love in business is all about relationships rather than transactions. *Shared values* - how often have you been offered a big contract, but you're doubtful about how your client would treat you? Of course, business is not all a bowl of cherries. Sometimes you must deliver a difficult message to a colleague or employee or let people go. I call it *tough love*. You can still be caring, but you have to challenge directly and honestly.

As I've travelled on my journey embracing love in business, I've been inspired and enlightened by some fantastic authors who have taught me so much. I strongly recommend these books, as well as *The Five Dysfunctions of a Team* that I referenced earlier:

- *'Love is Just Damn Good Business'* by Steve Farber
- *'Loveworks'* by Brian Sheehan and Kevin Roberts
- *'Firms of Endearment'* by Raj Sisodia, Jag Sheth and David Wolfe
- *'Loving Your Business'* by Debbie King
- *'The Lovemarks Effect'* by Kevin Roberts

I passionately believe that developing, nurturing and living by the values of love in business is not only personally fulfilling but also commercially successful. I hope these thoughts and tips will help build your own 6 Star Business, and I wish you well.

[1] Elkington. J (Author) (1999). Cannibals with Forks: The Triple Bottom Line of 21st Century Business. Capstone.

[2] Wolfe. B, Sheth. J, Sisodia. R (Authors) (2003). Firms of Endearment: How World-Class Companies Profit from Passion and Purpose. Pearson FT Press. In this book, the authors used this model to measure twenty-eight corporations over a two-year period, eighteen of which were publicly listed. These widely loved public companies outperformed the S&P 500 by huge margins, over ten, five, and three-year time horizons. The public 'FoEs' returned 1,026 per cent for investors over the ten years ending June 30, 2006, compared to 122 per cent for the S&P 500; that's more than an 8-to-1 ratio!

ALAN WICK

Alan Wick is a renowned business coach and management consultant who has specialised in supporting growth-minded entrepreneurs for 20 years. Prior to this, he spent 25 years founding, scaling and selling businesses nationally and internationally. This experience has been key to helping his clients take their businesses where they want them to go (one of the companies he led won two Queen's Awards for Export and one Queen's Award for Innovation).

Alan guides small business owners by sharing his experiences and stories, helping them overcome their obstacles to reach their goals more quickly and with less stress, through a rigorous process underpinned with love. This leads to a future with increased profits and impact, without working longer hours. He is purpose-led, values influence over profit, and does business in a way that balances commerce and compassion, putting long-term sustainability ahead of short-term profit.'

You can reach Alan via:

lovebusiness@alanwick.com

www.alanwick.com

www.facebook.com/alanwicklovebusiness

www.instagram.com/alancwick

www.linkedin.com/in/alanwick

https://twitter.com/alanwick

CHAPTER TWELVE

HOW TO PLAN AND ACHIEVE YOUR LEGACY

Let me take you back to 2015. I'm in my office holding crisis talks with my business partner. We're urgently discussing, in low tones, what a toxic member of staff has just told us. This member of staff was someone we had trusted. Someone we thought was operating in line with who we were as a business.

But from what they said, it was clear they weren't! The comments had ripped the lid off a much bigger can of worms in the business.

So here we were, fourteen years into the journey of running and building a business, holding crisis talks, with everything on the cusp of being completely wiped away. As we talked, it became abundantly clear that our legacy was one of destroyed relationships.

We left the meeting and had a good reflection on who we were as individuals. Then, when we came back, we held up our hands and said, "This isn't okay." How we were doing things just wasn't acceptable.

It was during that moment of crisis that a conscious decision point came about. It forced us to ask if we could actually do something with this business? Do we *want* to do something with this business?

We made a conscious decision to create a thriving environment that would support our staff and our families. To build a profitable business that would do only the things with which we felt in sync.

We also acknowledged that this process would take time...

Legacy is an Ancient Human Tradition

Humans have always built great things over long time frames and that were meant to stand the test of time and announce, "We were here!"

It took an estimated 100,000 men twenty years to build the Great Pyramid at Giza. Unknown craftsmen constructed Stonehenge in England over 1,500 years, with the central 'bluestones' quarried 150 miles away in Wales.

Here in Australia, the Indigenous stories of the Dreamtime date back 65,000 years. That's a long time to maintain a body of work!

Legacy is in your blood. It's a natural human impulse to create with legacy in mind. Fortunately, your business doesn't have to be a magnificent monument that gets passed down from generation to generation for it to be your legacy.

Legacy is simply success in the eyes of the people that are building it. So if you achieve what you set out to achieve, that's your legacy.

What do you have to offer the world that would benefit the broadest possible community? Can you change the lives of the people you serve? Can you achieve a more significant impact with the time you have here on Earth? Can you build something that helps people even after you are gone?

Why Legacy Goes Wrong

Sometimes your legacy will lie in the opposite direction to current operational pressures. You have to be clear about the legacy you want to create; otherwise, short term decisions can lead you further away.

In my business, things have gone wrong when I've stopped working in line with who I am and with my values. What throws things out when things go wrong is operating out of sync with your values.

I am a civil engineer by qualification, so I'm pretty cut and dry about how things work. Earlier in my career, I was uninterested in what people call 'soft skills'. I toiled under the tyranny of just being busy. I didn't have time to pause work and analyse my values. I was too busy to consider who I was as a person.

I've since realised these 'soft skills' are actually core universal principles and the foundation of business success.

Understanding who you are at your core is a position of strength. That's the foundation upon which you build everything else.

It's Never too Late

What if your business is already mature? What if, like me, you're more than a decade in when you suffer a crisis of purpose?

There are certainly people out there that are infused with purpose from the get-go. You see extraordinary teenagers, the future Zuckerbergs of this world, that are doing phenomenal work. But for the vast majority of us, gaining clarity on your legacy takes time.

You need the perspective of a life lived, to some degree. You need to go on a journey before you can start to look back.

So, how do you go about it?

Step 1: Quieten Down the Noise

To begin this process, you first need to quieten down the noise in the business. First, ask yourself: what's your long-term target for helping people? Think outside of where you are today, between eight and thirty-five years into the future.

Short term pressures fade into insignificance on those time frames. As a result, the noise of business operations becomes less deafening.

Step 2: Understand Your Numbers

Next, it's time to get absolute clarity on what you can do today to generate the results you want tomorrow. Then establish some initial priorities with your long-term goals in mind.

Initial progress helps to validate your new or refined business direction across your leadership team. Without this step, short term pressures will jump back to the fore.

Step 3: Craft Your Vision

Once your business stabilises, you can layer on top:

- The vision of where you're going as an organisation
- A plan to get there

This step starts with understanding your values and who you are. First, identify your core beliefs. Then ask, why exactly do you exist as a business? And what are you doing to bring that to life?

Identify a goal with at least a ten-year horizon and work back from there. What are things going to look like three years from now?

Where do you need to be one year from now? Finally, what are you doing in the next ninety days to bring your new plan to life?

Ninety days is the optimum time frame for tactical implementation. In effect, you are breaking down your ten-year vision into ninety-day sprints.

Step 4: Monitor Progress

Meet regularly with your leadership team (which could be just you, in the beginning) for ninety minutes a week. First, step out of the business of day-to-day hustle. Then ask are you on track with the numbers you identified in Step 2? Do you need to make any course corrections?

In these meetings, you're not looking at last quarter's profit. Instead, you may be looking at how many sales calls you've made this week. Or how many support tickets were closed. Measurable metrics that check you did the things that will bring your plan to life.

Your Decision-Making Litmus Test

Your legacy plan becomes your decision-making litmus test for all new opportunities that pass your desk. It's infinitely easier to keep your business on track with your legacy plan in place.

Imagine for a moment that you're in an Olympic rowing boat. In every decision, you ask: will this help the boat go faster? Will this decision move you towards your legacy or away from it?

My legacy plan is a two-page business plan, not a five-fold compendium gathering dust on a shelf. Instead, it's a single laminated page printed double-sided. I carry it around and into meetings and ask my leadership team to do the same.

That document helps us make decisions that are congruent with who we are and where we are going. It helps us avoid shiny object syndrome. It helps us avoid dual focus.

Results in Practice

I have a client in the alternative energy space. It's a reasonably sized business with operations across Australia. They had fallen in love with some engineering tools but weren't clear on how to use them.

Over the last year, we've helped them gain clarity on who they are as an organisation. As a result, they've expanded their focus from engineering to alternative energy as a whole.

In 2021, during a global pandemic, they experienced 50% revenue growth with around a 40% increase in profit. This success has come from gaining clarity on where the business is going.

The client broke out of a cycle of endless meetings about meetings and began to deliver on things. Not only is the business more successful, but the owners are sleeping at night too! They are no longer lying awake at night worrying about the business. The people in the business have more fulfilling work. That's a far more significant impact than profitability alone.

Are the people in your business having positive conversations about coming to work? Do they talk enthusiastically to anyone who will listen? That's how you know you're on the right track.

Putting your values at the core of things means you'll attract employees who share those values. Hiring nightmares will become a thing of the past. You'll have the right people on the bus, every time.

Summary

If you're feeling unsatisfied or uncertain about the long-term legacy of your business, then you're on the cusp of making significant changes. It's never too late to change. You should be getting satisfaction and joy from your business. Life is short. Never compromise on this.

It doesn't matter how old your business is. As long as you've got the desire to get clear on who you are and where you're going, then you can build a legacy.

As I write these words in 2021, my daughter has just started work at my business. When she began, I stood back for a moment and thought, "wow" I didn't consciously set out to do this. But I LOVE that she is working here. The fact that someone close to me who wasn't even alive when I started the business is now working here fires me out of bed in the morning.

That's my version of legacy. Yours will be different.

A legacy is part of a 6 Star Business.

A 6 Star Business is built to stand the test of time.

Think big, plan often, and stay true to your values.

ANTHONY WOOD, Certified EOS Implementer

After more than twenty-five years of building several successful and some not so successful companies, Anthony is tapping into his passion for helping entrepreneurs live their ideal lives. It's been a long journey that started when he co-founded a company called Imei in 2000 with a trusted business partner. After many years of sustained growth, he and his business partner stepped back, leaving it in the hands of a new CEO.

Unfortunately, things didn't work out. To cut a long story short, Anthony and his co-founder took back the reins and worked with a professional EOS Implementer. They embedded the Entrepreneurial Operating System and ultimately turned things around.

He was hooked; seeing how impactful EOS was in his own business has led him to offer entrepreneurial leadership teams a blueprint for success that will bring clarity, instil accountability and enhance their health as a team so, in turn, they can strengthen their organisation.

You can reach Anthony via:

0411880994

anthony.wood@eosworldwide.com

www.eosworldwide.com/anthony-wood

CHAPTER THIRTEEN

MOVING TOWARDS THE FIRE: THE POWER OF COURAGEOUS, WHOLEHEARTED LEADERSHIP

I was five months pregnant with my first child when I took on my first CEO position.

It seemed like my dream job and the pinnacle of my career. To be able to lead a charity I had supported and loved since my teens. So I gave up another brilliant job and dived in.

During those four months, in the run-up to my maternity leave, I worked harder and longer than I had ever worked. I put my heart and soul into the role, determined to lay strong foundations before having my baby.

I succeeded in building an open, trusting culture after a painful period of restructuring had left a residue of fear amongst staff. I put into place an ambitious fundraising strategy, which exceeded its targets. I built strong relationships with my board of trustees and created thorough interim plans to cover my maternity leave.

But then - two weeks before my baby was due - we were hit with a big, external curveball that was outside of our control. We had to change the whole direction of the organisation, and huge decisions would need to be taken when I was due to be on the labour ward. Working with my senior team, we put in place decision-making processes and protocols. It was tough to delegate such weighty decisions, but there was no other option.

When I returned after my maternity leave, it was to a very different organisation. The finances had taken a massive hit during that period of change, and I had to pick up the pieces and work out what went wrong so that we could learn lessons. First, we needed to cut costs dramatically and devise a new strategy for the year ahead on a much-reduced budget. Then reassure the trustee board and manage the staff - whose trust in me had waned due to distance - through a profoundly unsettling period of uncertainty.

And all of this had to be done part-time while sleep-deprived from looking after a six-month-old baby. I remember looking at multiple budget spreadsheets and staffing restructure options late at night, feeding my son when he woke up at 1 am, and continuing to work after resettling him. Then sleeping for a few hours before starting all over again. It felt overwhelming.

It was not the first time I had faced a crisis as a senior leader, but it was the first time I had to face one as a CEO and a new mother, and while feeling like an outsider after a long period of absence.

Courageous Leadership in Moments of Crisis

I believe 6 Star business leaders need to be courageous in such moments of crisis.

But the courage required in those moments is not about putting on a brave face. It is about being wholehearted. It is about vulnerability and empathy and creating a culture where it is normal to talk about - and show - emotions. Where people are heard and then empowered to come up with solutions.

I hear leaders describe their fears of 'opening up a can of worms' or 'making it worse'. What if they cry? What if they get angrier?

These are normal fears to have. Difficult emotions are, well, difficult. It can be uncomfortable and unsettling to hear others' pain or anger. Especially if some of it is directed at us or if we feel unable to change the situation causing the anger or pain, as I did.

But, if we do not attend to difficult feelings and fears, they intensify and spill over. And later, the ignored feelings and resulting behaviours - and their impact on the broader team - take far more time and energy to address.

So I drew on my ten+ years of mediation experience and did the following things in response to the crisis:

- I created space - regularly - for staff to express their fears and feelings, both one-to-one and in team meetings. I took time to understand their feelings and the needs beneath them.
- I was transparent with everything I was able to share and honest about anything I wasn't. I clearly explained the severity of the situation, the costs we had to cut, that the new structure was unknown and that all our roles were potentially at risk.
- I was honest about my own mistakes and regrets, my questions and dilemmas, and my feelings. I remember a moment in a team meeting when I shared that my role was at high risk. I cried unexpectedly. It was an uncomfortable moment, but it modelled the vulnerability I was asking of others. To be open about emotions rather than bottling them up or having corridor conversations.
- I involved everyone in re-imagining the organisation within the tight budget restrictions. I shared my hope that together we

could devise the best possible outcome for the organisation and its stakeholders and save as many jobs as possible.

Courageous Leadership creates Courageous Teams

I was blown away by the determination, positivity and innovation that everyone brought to the table. Despite the chronic uncertainty around who would have a role in the new organisation, they pulled together as one team.

Wholehearted leadership results in loyalty to you and the organisation, even in the toughest of times.

Recent research from the University of Edinburgh Business School (2020) found that empathy motivates employees to go beyond the call of duty:

"...Empathy from direct supervisors/line managers, and a simple human acknowledgement of the challenges being faced by employees, motivated employees to not only readily accept pandemic-induced organisational change but also extend more support/help to their peers."

Because my team had received empathy and an acknowledgement of their fears and other emotions, they were able to accept the need for drastic cuts and creatively problem-solve. Of course, there were inevitable wobbles along the way, but we nipped those in the bud through good listening and attention to the feelings involved.

Courageous Leadership Through Vulnerability and Empathy

"Most people, if not everyone, has something in them that's loveable, and they have something that they're scared about." Dr Vivek Murphy (US Surgeon General and loneliness researcher)

1. Lean into Vulnerability

Brené Brown defines vulnerability as the emotion we experience during times of uncertainty, risk, and emotional exposure. So engaging with vulnerability - which is crucial to courageous leadership - means leaning into the situations that make us feel uncertain, at-risk or emotionally exposed. I think of it as moving towards the fire.

From twenty+ years of mediating conflict, I know that skirting around the toughest issues leads to lukewarm relationships, mediocre teams and - sometimes - toxic conflict. Only through moving towards the difficult conversations, the painful emotions, the feedback we're dreading can we build courageous, creative, resilient teams.

It is never comfortable to do this. But it's in this discomfort that we often experience the most profound learning, growth and connection, to ourselves and others.

2. Practice Empathy

There are many, many definitions of empathy out there. My working definition, based on twenty years of developing it in others, is:

'Showing wholehearted, non-judgemental attention to the perspectives, feelings and needs of another person.'

Empathy is contagious, and it is good for business. If people experience it from their managers, they will reciprocate it and pass it on to their peers. And they will want to go the extra mile for the business.

Empathy is simple but deeply powerful. Just taking the time to ask your team 'how are you coping?' and listening compassionately to the responses, without judging or trying to change them, will build resilience and loyalty.

Practising Vulnerability and Empathy: A Take-away

Try using my 3Ns - *Notice, Name and Normalise* strong feelings - in yourself and others:

- **NOTICE**

  Try to notice how people are feeling and actively encourage the expression of difficult emotions, even if they make you uncomfortable. (The feelings wheel below might help you or others to identify and articulate feelings.)

  Try to slow down and observe yourself too. What are the signs of rising emotion in you?

- **NAME**

  Name the feelings you hear expressed so people feel heard and understood. Reflecting back on the anxiety, anger, and sadness people are feeling is simple, but it goes a long way towards calming their emotional state. 'So you've said you're feeling really upset and worried.'

Don't try to change the feeling or take the sting out of it - this will only cause further frustration. Instead, just acknowledge and accept the feelings you've heard.

Try to pinpoint your own emotions too. Externalising them can be helpful - try writing them down or speaking them aloud to someone. (Again, my feelings wheel below will help.)

- **NORMALISE**

People often feel ashamed to express difficult emotions. So it's important to normalise these emotions, for example, by saying 'it is completely understandable to feel anxious at a time like this, and I'm glad you can express this to me'. This helps create a psychologically safe space.

Practice self-empathy, too - remember that you are human and will sometimes feel difficult emotions.

Conclusion

My son is now eight years old. I asked him recently if he knows what courage means. His response was: "Of course I do! It means to encourage someone."

People often associate courage with bravery in battle. But the root of the word courage is heart ('cor' in Latin). It's about vulnerability and speaking what's in our hearts and on our minds.

And 'en-couragement' is about strengthening others. But not so they can fight well. It means 'to hearten'. To give heart to someone and provide them with hope and confidence to do or say something important.

So my son is right. I set up Courage Lab to en-courage leaders and teams. To give them the courage, hope and skills to speak from the heart, with honesty and empathy.

This kind of courage isn't easy. It is rare, but it can be learnt. And it is contagious. It starts with small acts, but it grows – in us and in others. We start to realise what is possible. And we end up with courageous cultures, where vulnerability, empathy and stepping into discomfort becomes the norm.

This kind of courage is desperately needed at the moment as we face continuing uncertainty, grief and difficult choices.

It takes a 6 Star business to develop this kind of courage in its leaders and teams.

I hope that this chapter en-courages you to move towards the fire.

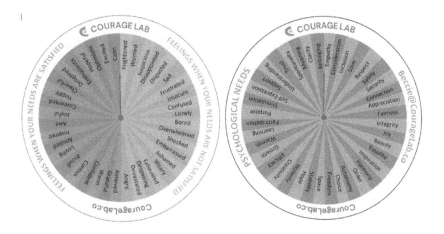

BECCIE D'CUNHA

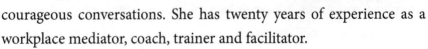

Beccie is the founder of Courage Lab, which supports leaders and teams to have courageous conversations. She has twenty years of experience as a workplace mediator, coach, trainer and facilitator.

Beccie is an experienced leader, having held several CEO and Director level positions in charities and small businesses, including one of the UK's first workplace mediation companies. She has a strong track record of building courageous, resilient, high-performing teams and leading organisations through change, crisis and uncertainty.

Beccie loves doing deep work with leaders and teams who are courageous enough to do the inner and outer work needed to build courageous cultures. As an expert facilitator, coach, trainer and mediator, she creates courageous spaces that inspire and enable vulnerability, hope and empathy, even in the toughest of situations.

She is a Lumina Spark and Enneagram practitioner and uses these personality models to help individuals and teams to develop emotional intelligence, empathy and strong relationships.

Beccie provides:

- Courageous Leaders group coaching programmes
- Coaching for leadership teams or individuals - in personality styles, conflict or leadership
- Team-building workshops - using Lumina Spark psychometric
- Skills workshops

- Mediation for teams or individuals in conflict

You can reach Beccie via:

www.couragelab.co

https://www.linkedin.com/in/becciedcunha/

beccie@couragelab.co

CHAPTER FOURTEEN

HOW COMMUNITY SUPPORTS
A 6 STAR BUSINESS

"Congratulations!" Vincent, my agent said, as I held the faded and cracked receiver of the shared payphone in my digs to my ear. "You've got your first professional acting job. The director of 'Jack and The Beanstalk' wants you."

"'Fleshcreep', the villain?" I asked tentatively.

"Unfortunately, no," Vincent replied. "They've gone with a semi-famous TV sitcom actor for 'Fleshcreep', though they do want you to be the understudy. They've also offered you 'The Beanman'. And 'The Giant'. Still, it's your first job, and it's twelve weeks of work at full Equity pay. I'll post the contract to you tomorrow. Sign and send it back, and I'll give you all the details."

"YES!" I exclaimed as I punched the air in delight after hanging up the phone.

I might not have landed Fleshcreep, the part I really wanted, but my dreams of being a professional actor were now a reality.

The four-week rehearsal period passed in a flash, and before I knew it, we were playing to packed houses, matinee and evening, at the brand-spanking-new Basildon Towngate Theatre in Essex, England.

"This really is the life!" I said to myself as I sauntered into the winter sun-drenched winter foyer of the theatre one Saturday morning six weeks into the run, uncharacteristically early for the matinee show.

"Good job, you're early today, Pete," said Peter John, the RADA-trained actor who was bringing down the house every performance as the pantomime dame, "You're on as Fleshcreep. Brett's called in sick."

"Ha, ha! Pull the other one. It's got bells on it.", I laughed in reply.

"No. Seriously. Get yourself backstage as quick as you can."

My jubilant mood plummeted like a black stone to the pit of my stomach.

It was ages since I'd learned Fleshcreep's lines.

I'd never rehearsed the sword fighting scene with 'Jack'.

I didn't have a costume (and Brett was a lot shorter than me).

And I barely knew how to do my own stage makeup, let alone the complicated hour-long process I saw Brett go through before every show.

How on earth could this be anything other than an embarrassing, humiliating, unmitigated disaster for me?

If I thought the four-week rehearsal period had gone by in a flash, the three hours before the curtain went up was a whirlwind of script revision, stage fight rehearsing, costume fitting and sitting in a makeup chair as I was passed between the creatives and backstage crew all busily focused on doing their bit as best they could. At times it felt like it was all happening at the same time.

"Act one, beginners. This is your act one beginners call," came the announcement from the stage manager over the PA in the green room.

With every step feeling like I was wearing the lead-lined boots of a deep-sea diving suit, I trudged the short distance from the sanctuary and safety of the green room to stage left. It was from here that I would make my entrance early in the first scene.

"I wonder if this is how the Christians felt before they were pushed out into the Colosseum," I thought.

And then I heard it.

My cue line.

Nothing for it.

Deep breath.

One foot in front of the other.

The bright light of my follow spot found me as soon as I was on the stage.

"BOOOOOOOOOOOOOOOOOOOO!!!!!!!!!!!" screamed 150 school children at the top of their lungs.

I WAS Fleshcreep!

Before I knew it, the last bow had been taken at the curtain call and, with the applause and excited shouts of the children fading to a recent memory, I practically leapt into the green room - adrenaline and endorphins still coursing through my body.

Judging by all the smiles, laughter, high-fives and hugs, I wasn't the only one on a natural high! We'd done it.

WE had done it.

Because I couldn't have pulled off Fleshcreep without the group, the other actors, the makeup artists or the wardrobe team or without the last second pep talk from the director.

And that's the thing about being in a community. It has the power to drive you forwards. To challenge you to do something you think you can't do. To hold you accountable. To help and support you.

I recognise two types of community that can help a business be 6 Star: Peer and Customer.

Peer Communities

If building a business was easy, everyone would do it, and the failure rates wouldn't be so high!

The reality is that any meaningful endeavour in any aspect of life is challenging and requires us to adapt and grow; develop new skills and improve old ones; go where we've never gone before - physically, mentally and emotionally.

Jim Rohn said, "Everyone should strive to be a millionaire. Not for the money in the bank but for who you have to become in the process."

And I say, "Business is the ideal playground for personal development."

So, you may not realise it, but that's the real reason you started your business... to accelerate your transformation as a human!

And that journey of transformation, like any journey, is both more likely and more fun when you're with others on the same journey.

So if you're not in a community of business owners who are on the same wavelength as you, I strongly urge you to find one and or create one.

I've done both and am currently a member of two peer communities. I found the Connect Collaborative, and I created the 6

Star Business Community. They each serve a different purpose for me, though that could be the subject of another chapter.

It's a lot easier to join an existing community, but if you can't find one that gels, I highly recommend the Mighty Networks platform and training to create your own.

That's what we did with the 6 Star Business Community. We realised that many of the people we talked to on the 6 Star Business podcast were people we wanted to stay connected to and be in a community. And as the common denominator was '6 Star Business', it made sense for us to create a community where our podcast guests could connect and share their journey with other people who were thinking about life and business in a similar way.

Don't underestimate the work involved in setting up your own community, but the rewards are great - not least of which is the growth you'll experience as you lead the community.

Customer Communities

I'd go so far as to say that a customer community is essential for your business to be 6 Star.

And I'm not talking about just whacking up YANFAG (Yet ANother FAcebook Group!)

The world doesn't need more Facebook Groups.

It needs more privacy-oriented, advert and distraction-free, curated communities built on platforms that engender and encourage the sort of connections and relationships on which we as humans thrive.

Here are some to get you started on your research (at wildly different price points):

Mighty Networks - https://mightynetworks.com
Circle - https://circle.so/
BuddyBoss - https://www.buddyboss.com/
Tribe - https://tribe.so/
Disciple - https://www.disciplemedia.com/
Hivebrite - https://hivebrite.com/
Influitive - https://influitive.com/

Without a customer community, you are relying on the individual relationship between each customer and your business. A single tie is easily broken.

A customer community allows your customers to easily connect and build relationships with other people seeking the same transformation as them. Isn't that why any of us buy anything, to experience some sort of transformation?

And, as mentioned earlier, the transformation all your customers are looking for will be more likely and more fun when they're with others seeking the same transformation.

That web of connections creates strong relational bonds, which are harder to break and translate to increased loyalty to your brand and business.

There are four other main reasons for you to establish a customer community:

- It' forces' you to stay focused on the excellence inherent in being 6 Star because your customers can easily talk to each other.

- It creates a low-cost way for potential customers to experience your brand.
- Potential customers will be in the community alongside existing customers who, as you're a 6 Star Business, should all be strong advocates for your brand and business.
- Being so close to your customers allows you to get immediate, direct input from them about additional products and services they're looking for, some of which might be valuable for you to create.

Summary (or TL;DR if you're used to that!)

1. Ultimately, you are in business to grow as a human.
2. The transformation inherent in that growth is more likely and more fun in a community - "No man is an island."
3. Your customers are seeking transformation, and point 2. is true for them too.
4. A customer community effectively 'forces' you to be a 6 Star Business.

Finally, if you resonate with the values, principles and ethos of a 6 Star Business, you're welcome to a free one-month guest pass of the 6 Star Business Community at https://guestpass.6starbusiness. community.

We'd love to see you there.

ABOUT THE AUTHOR

PETER DALY-DICKSON, Co-founder
& Co-host, 6 Star Business Podcast &
Community

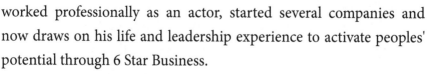

Peter was brought up in Hong Kong. He initially studied computers, trained and worked professionally as an actor, started several companies and now draws on his life and leadership experience to activate peoples' potential through 6 Star Business.

Peter is a husband and [step]dad to four kids, and he is a runner - 31st October 2021 marked seven years of running at least two miles every day.

He currently lives in Coventry, England, loves going to music festivals and enjoys exploring the UK in a 1994 touring caravan that he and his wife renovated during COVID lockdown in 2021.

You can reach Peter via:

https://www.linkedin.com/in/peterdalydickson/

CHAPTER FIFTEEN

HAVE YOU CONSIDERED WHETHER YOUR MARKETING IS ETHICAL?

Puzzled faces looked back at me as I uttered the words, and a bead of shame trickled down my head, as I realised at that moment why the discipline of marketing, for some, has such a bad name.

As the charity's Trustee with marketing expertise, it was my job to challenge ideas and activities and offer advice on how things could be improved. We were having a virtual event on this occasion, no less, as the pandemic had just kicked in. Then the discussion around the table turned to how to drum up additional interest in the event to secure some much-needed ticket revenue for the charity.

"How could we engineer an impression of scarcity," I said, knowing full well that there's nothing like a bit of FOMO (fear of missing out) to get people to open up their wallets.

It was at that moment that the decades of focusing on short-term commercial results came home to roost. I realised that I had become too used to the idea of being a servant to owners and faceless shareholders rather than the customers who we were meant to serve. I was involved with the charity precisely because I wanted to put my skills to good use for a cause and purpose entirely intended to benefit people. Yet here I was, doing it a disservice by projecting unethical marketing practices upon it.

Now, I may be over-dramatising somewhat by putting my actions in line with some of the big corporate villains of our time like Bernie Madoff, but I've always been fascinated by the psychology behind why good people do bad things. A couple of the psychological forces lurking behind my actions undoubtedly included 'tunnel vision' and 'winner-takes-all competition.'

Fundamentally though, what I learnt from this experience, was that if you want to be a 6 Star Leader, you need to get used to spotting, calling out and crucially, creating a culture where ethical marketing is recognised, respected and expected as the benchmark. When my Co-Founder and I started our own business, this is exactly why we put ethical marketing right at the heart of it.

> *"Integrity is doing the right thing,*
> *even when no one is watching."*
> - C.S. Lewis

So what is ethical marketing?

In its simplest form, ethical marketing is helpful and inspiring, not manipulative or intrusive. Beyond that, it is the bedrock that can support, communicate and champion a business's purpose.

Right now, across the world, businesses are embracing the need to act sustainably. However, while that decision will often be inspired by business owners who fundamentally believe in the power of business being a force for good, consumers are also being influenced by the increasing demand for such behaviour.

In a 2021 survey of 2000+ UK adults aged 18+, by YouGov on behalf of Deloitte*, it emerged that nearly one in three in consumers claimed to have stopped purchasing certain brands or products because they had ethical or sustainability-related concerns about them.

This trend has not gone unnoticed by the financial investors of this world too. For SDGs (Sustainable Development Goals) and ESG (Environment, Social and Governance) factors have increasingly come to the fore, as the positive link between financial performance and strong corporate ESG policies and practices are increasingly being supported by a growing body of evidence.

So why is it that a business discipline - marketing - which has so much potential for championing positive messages and change, is still viewed with such cynicism?

I'm not surprised this cynicism persists. And marketing is often an afterthought for how one should act like a 6 Star Business. While there's a broad acceptance that marketing can be a vehicle for transmitting an ethical business message, often there's a failure to appreciate the unethical nature of the tactics or even psychology behind those messages.

Even B-Corp, the world's leading movement and private certification of for-profit companies that want to balance profit with people and the planet, hasn't yet considered marketing as part of its extensive criteria for what makes a 'business for good'. The comprehensive impact assessment, which is a key part of the certification procedure, is hugely commendable and puts the onus on the business to thoroughly evaluate the ethical nature of its treatment, policies and contributions towards workers, community, customers and the environment. Still, within that sphere, the implications of marketing are somewhat left out.

We stand at an exciting crossroads, in which the entire reputation of marketing could go either way. A 2021 study by Merkle** revealed that while 44% of US adult internet users said it feels too invasive when brands use their data in advertising, 50% said it helped them discover products and services that interest them. It's entirely within the capability of 6 Star Business leaders to ensure the majority view increasingly becomes the latter through a determined commitment towards ethical marketing.

> *"The best marketing doesn't feel like marketing"*
> **- Tom Fishburne**

Ethical marketing in practice.

The 4P's of marketing are one of the cornerstones of business theory that are as relevant today as they were when first proposed by E. Jerome McCarthy in 1960 and later popularised by Phillip Kotler. While the decade of the naughties has brought with it many challenges to the number and content of those 4P's, the core quartet of Product, Price, Place and Promotion is a valuable prism through which to examine how a business might choose to market itself ethically.

Product

How well are your products linked to your purpose? With the rise of ethical consumerism, people increasingly want to feel assured that their purchasing is sustainable and ethically produced. The brands that genuinely and coherently link their purpose and values with the products or services they sell will benefit from that consistency of approach through buy-in and loyalty from consumers and employees alike. Honesty about your ingredients or product components, and transparency around your supply chain, for example, can then be confidently communicated as both product and brand benefits, thus setting you apart from those competitors jumping onboard a topical bandwagon.

Price

Is psychological pricing ok, just because everyone else does it? We're all familiar with the concept of charm pricing and will, in most cases, have accepted it as a social norm, but the practice of making prices seem cheaper than they are, through the tactical use of 99 pence or cent price tags, exists only to benefit the seller. There has even been research*** to show how reverse-engineered price hikes (e.g. $5.99 - $6.00) are powerful enough to impact an individual's motivation to stop smoking. Ultimately, using a clear and transparent price point is helpful to the consumer and enables them to evaluate the said product or service best, based on its merits.

Place

My competitors are advertising on Facebook, so why shouldn't I? Where you sell or promote can say a lot about your brand and the values it upholds. For example, it became an increasingly common and obvious choice for brands to steer clear of advertising across the new, right-wing news channel, GB News. But there have also been cases where brands have taken less obvious and bolder stances against advertising behemoths, such as Facebook.

In this case, what started as a trickle in early 2020 from ethically minded small businesses, unhappy with the social media giant's handling of misinformation and hate speech, led to boycotts from some of the world's largest brands. In the case of big spenders Adidas & Reebok, it meant temporarily pulling $12.4m of ad money and developing global guidelines for holding "ourselves and every one of our partners accountable for creating and maintaining safe environments."

Promotion

How could we engineer an impression of scarcity? The last 'P' is an area, particularly in a world where so much marketing has gone online, fraught with potential for unethical marketing. Some of the more common practices you might be familiar with include artificial scarcity, which I nearly fell into the trap of in my earlier story and is all the easier to execute in a digital environment. Think 'three people are also viewing this item' and 'you have thirty seconds to complete this transaction'. Both tactics are common in the travel and ticketing trades and deliberately play to our loss aversion and force people to make uninformed snap decisions.

Another common tactic you might have seen is lead magnets, in which a business will use the lure of a free item to draw a customer in. Unfortunately, the reality is often an equal exchange of, for example, a pdf guide for a customer's data. When fully transparent that this is a value exchange and not 'free', and where it's clear how a customer can opt-out of data, the practice can be fair and ethical, but where it's not, it's simply manipulative.

Case Study

Soda Folk is a fast-growing soft drinks company that make authentic sodas that are 100% natural and made with the finest ingredients. From the moment their Founder, Ken, had the idea to put the guy who ran his local bike repair shop on the can of their popular Root Beer, Chief Soda Maker, Simon Waterfall, saw the power of bringing to life their natural and ethical credentials beyond just promotion. "It just made so much sense to deliver our three core values of 'Good Soda, Good Folk, Good Deeds' through our product. So many competitors have a philanthropic angle they tag on as a communications tactic. By contrast, we are so serious about it; we put people on our cans and hero them across the UK. We don't want to pretend we alone can save the planet; instead, we want to recognise the amazing people that walk amongst us and celebrate their good deeds in the hope that it feels relatable and resonates on an emotive level with our drinkers."

> *"People don't buy what you do; they buy why you do it."*
> **- Simon Sinek**

So next time you're evaluating your marketing, I urge you to take a step back and think: is this fundamentally conveying my brand's core values and purpose in a helpful and inspiring way and are the tactics we're employing ethical?

A 6 Star Business should be able to look itself in the mirror and feel confident that it enables potential customers to make purchase decisions based on genuine interest, relevance and desire. For if built on that foundation, not only will your customers be far more inclined to trust, repeat purchase and recommend your brand, but you, your team, and the people you surround yourself with will feel prouder of the business you've built.

*https://www2.deloitte.com/uk/en/pages/consumer-business/articles/sustainable-consumer.html

**https://www.emarketer.com/content/consumer-attitudes-toward-digital-advertising-2021

***https://tobaccocontrol.bmj.com/content/23/6/501

ABOUT THE AUTHOR

CHRIS THORNHILL, Co-Founder & CEO - **Growth Animals**

Chris's animal personality is a Falcon, which means he's imaginative, decisive, and can have a slightly short attention span. He's also on a mission to clean up marketing and put ethics right at the forefront.

Chris spent the first fifteen years of his career launching and growing brands across the globe for high profile businesses like AutoTrader, Carlsberg and Goodwood.

After joining the charity Dementia Support, as a Trustee, he was inspired to take his experience and values to the broader community.

When Chris and Co-Founder, Jen Bayford, set up Growth Animals at the height of the pandemic, they were inspired by the trifecta of helping SMEs through their extensive brand experience, giving back to society through charitable time and donations every time they won business and the opportunity to educate people how marketing can be practised ethically.

Growth Animals' mission is to help businesses grow their bottom line AND positive impact through marketing that is helpful and inspiring, not manipulative or intrusive.

You can reach Chris via:

chris@growthanimals.com

www.growthanimals.com

07711791421

https://www.linkedin.com/in/christopherthornhill/

Find out your animal personality:

https://growthanimals.com/about/

CHAPTER SIXTEEN

6 STAR SERVICE
- IT'S 10/10 OR NOTHING!

Would you love to have no price competition, or at least reduce it to the barest minimum?

How would it change your business model if you didn't have to compete on price and predict your margins and revenue?

If your team never had to worry about discounting and price matching, how would that change your culture, and how do you train them? What would it do to team morale?

Every product and service has a #1 supplier, be it global or local, and this supplier rarely, if ever, needs to discount (have you ever seen a sale at the Apple store?). Their uniqueness separates them from their competition, they have the best customers and the best team, yet they operate in the same market as their competition.

So what sets them apart? They obsess over their customers and not over their competition, and they enjoy a level of customer loyalty that most only can dream of.

Let's look at some critical distinctions of customer loyalty, mainly the strength. Is it fragile or unshakable? Is it purchased or earned? Is it a moving strategy or a predictable process? If your customer loyalty is geared to a loyalty program or card it isn't a 6 Star business loyalty. If you turned off your loyalty programs, what would happen?

If sales stay strong, you don't need to discount; you can turn it off and redirect the margins into more significant returns. But, if your revenue falls or price becomes an issue, you don't have genuine customer loyalty, you have a discount program, and you always have to buy your customers.

Why 6 Star?

Why is it so critical to embrace 6 Star thinking? Some managers say it's not profitable; their market won't support it. But is it the market, or are they good enough to operate there? Some do well by discounting, but they are structured for it and choose to work there. Most just fight it out one transaction at a time. However, a 6 Star business thinks; differently they say it doesn't cost; it pays and keeps on paying. A 6 Star business has a core belief that the customer is the most significant long-term asset, requiring an investment in team and culture to fulfil their promise of service excellence.

Competitive businesses see the customer as a means to an end and rarely sees long-term benefit in raising the bar. Review your credit card statement and think about what transactions were exceptional, and you will return. Approximately 85% are just OK businesses, most barely stand out, and some you will forget. The rest operate at a higher level of customer engagement and genuinely get the value of delivering a 6 Star experience.

The numbers don't lie.

A customer doesn't lie about excellent service. If you didn't deliver it, they would let you know.

Let's look at data from 74,816 real-time phone-based interviews my company Saguity, in Melbourne, performed. This extensive, highly accurate and diverse data reflects large and SME companies across multiple markets of products and services, B2B and B2C, large single based transactions and regular trade. All reflect the mindset of customers reflections on their service experience.

Your market probably fits in this data; it's relevant to you and profitable. We asked them how they would rate their experience out of ten with ten excellent and zero very poor. They were asked how their experience impacted their repeat business, referrals, value for money and wallet share.

The results are compelling and settle any myth that delivering an eight/ten (satisfaction) experience results in a strong balance sheet and substantial margins. The data reflects the power of a 10/10 experience score (6 Star) and how this builds a solid foundation for growth. If a company cannot clearly define its levels of customer appreciation, it's guessing and keeps spending money on new customer acquisition.

A 6 Star company that understands how to deliver 6 Star service will invest the minimum on marketing, and customer acquisition will result in business growth and not churn replacement. If you want to grow, improve retention, and reduce discounting, you must surpass the experience of every brand you and your customers know. Being good is not enough. You must be excellent and always stand out.

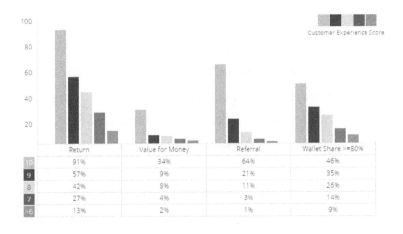

	Return	Value for Money	Referral	Wallet Share >=80%
10	91%	34%	64%	46%
9	57%	9%	21%	35%
8	42%	8%	11%	26%
7	27%	4%	3%	14%
>=6	13%	2%	1%	9%

Customer Experience Score

Client retention	Price acceptance	Word of mouth	Revenue optimisation
10/10 CX ensures more than 2X repeat business than a score of 8/10	10/10 CX protects price and massively reduces product discounting	10/10 CX delivers 6X more client referrals than a score of 8/10	10/10 CX delivers the highest level of exclusive supply (80%+)

Will 6 Star deliver on ROI?

Instead of being return **on** investment, 6 Star thinking is the return <u>of</u> investment, 100% Plus, it means every dollar you spend, you get multiple times back. The key is understanding how to protect your business's greatest asset and preserve the predictability of customer loyalty. If I'm buying your company, often the goodwill is the most valuable part of the business, or it should be. Buying goodwill is buying future revenue. Your past financials are the basis of goodwill, but I must accurately predict the future revenue of your customer base.

The data shows that the 10/10 (6 Star) experience is the most predictable, and retention, referrals, value for money and wallet share are critical elements of goodwill. 6 Star service doesn't just pay you today; it builds a powerful multiplier effect on the value of your goodwill in a business sale, which creates your asset.

Appreciation vs Satisfaction

Think of the people you genuinely value, trust and care about in your life. Those you respect and greatly appreciate. You have a potent heart connection to them; there's an emotional relationship. Now think about the OK people, the acquaintances who are friends, but you don't invite them for dinner. You are satisfied with them, they haven't done anything wrong, but they're just a head connection, and there's a degree of complacency.

Business is the same; we do business with companies we appreciate and others we are satisfied with. The former delivers us a 6 Star experience, the satisfied ones delivered as expected, no wow, just the basics. You will pay more for the appreciative experience, but the satisfied ones had better stack up on price. Customer Appreciation is a value-driven economy where we hold great relationships. Customer Satisfaction is a price-driven economy, driven by convenience and often short term or non-exclusive.

The 6 Star formula

When delivering a 10/10 experience based upon process and people, not opportunity and luck, there is a simple but powerful formula to apply. Seemingly simple it is challenging in the application, and the fundamental reason a 6 Star business is a rarity, not the norm. Like the eagle versus the seagull, one gets to choose the other fights over the scraps.

The 6 Star formula's objective is to achieve the optimal outcome in every possible situation. Gimmicks and quick deals do not achieve the objective; it's achieved by earning the right to be #1. "When it comes to being #1, there is no finish line".

There are three critical distinctions in the 6 Star formula, all must work in synergy, and one is the foundation of unshakable loyalty.

Theory + Experience + Prediction = Optimal Results. Let's break it down from a process perspective.

Theory – You must prove it; opinions aren't worth much. What theories drive the processes and systems in your business and are proven to deliver the optimal outcome? Do you have a documented and structured training platform ensuring everyone on your team has the knowledge base to train them to understand the delivery of a 10/10 experience? It **must** be customised to your business; you can't copy the pizza shops training process for a high-value product with multiple sales touchpoints. You must know about a 10/10 experience from an independent market perspective (your customer), then work backwards to the start, so you understand how the flow works. This requires accurate customer feedback defining the foundations of a 10/10 experience; you cannot determine this yourself. You cannot map the mind of your customer if you never research their beliefs. Your theory must stand up to scrutiny, and your customer is always the ultimate voice.

Experience – you can read a book on how to ride a bike. Experience is what matters, talk is cheap, and actions speak louder than words.

So, who are the experience champions in your business? Who do you trust to know what to do? If I was the most significant new customer of the year, which team members would you have in charge of my account ensuring I'm a 10/10? More importantly, who wouldn't you connect me with? Who needs more training to deliver excellence? How do you mentor, coach, and hold the new recruits accountable, so there is no chance of service standards slipping? More importantly, do you?

Prediction – your integrity and reputation are defined by what you say will happen. Have you ever been let down after being told what to expect from a supplier? Have you ever made a purchase trusting what the product will do, only to discover the opposite? On the other hand, have you experienced the delight when a significant supplier completely fulfils their promise and then goes beyond your expectations? Which one of the above has your unshakable loyalty?

A 6 Star business builds its reputation on its ability to accurately predict what will happen in your engagement. If anything unexpected occurs, you can predict they will be honest and tell you what they will do about it. The #1 businesses are #1 because of their ability to make and keep predictions. They can do this because they have the correct theory behind all the critical touchpoints on the customer journey. They also have all the right people on the bus knowing what to do to achieve a 10/10 experience.

Optimal Results

How do you define optimal results? How do you know if you're a 6 Star Business? Prediction is the key; if you can predict your cash flow, margins, sales conversion rates, repeat transactions, referrals, and team loyalty with a degree of accuracy. Then you have a powerful business worth a premium in the market, which will stand strong against the greatest of challenges. Any variation in these measurements indicates a potential breakdown of the 6-star process. A #1 business operates based on fundamentals and consistently measures them. They don't guess; they know.

A 6 Star business is not a destination; it's a never-ending journey. The road to success is paved with the inconvenience. It's not that you aren't aware of what a 6 Star business looks like; they are around us to observe and experience. Is it more a question of are you up for it? Do you believe that Optimal service is worth it, and do you have the culture to support it?

You can't buy your way there; you must earn the right. It's not a fancy marketing strategy; 6 Star is all about integrity. Different isn't always better, but better is always different.

To your success!

DARRELL HARDIDGE

Darrell is an industry-leading expert in optimising customer loyalty and understanding what drives a 10/10 customer experience. A 3x published author and bestseller, a professional speaker and trainer, the customer experience metric "Appreciation Certified" innovator. Darrell's company Saguity has interviewed over half a million end-user customers from hundreds of companies and identified the critical drivers behind creating a #1 company and a #1 team.

Darrell's mantra, "Different isn't always better, but better is always different", is the unique distinction behind how to define service excellence. While most companies try to be different to win business and compete on price, the true #1 companies learn how to be the best in service experience and compete on value. Darrell's team help companies to understand 'why they have loyalty and why they don't. This information is used to optimise internal processes and team training.

There is always a #1 company in every product and service, local, state or country. Knowing why they are #1 from an independent customer perspective is a critical part of their secret. Saguity's experience in researching #1 companies enables Darrell's knowledge in CX to be a powerful strategy for quality companies seeking an edge in their market.

CHAPTER SEVENTEEN

CREATE A 6 STAR PRE-SALES EXPERIENCE BY TELLING YOUR STORY

It's 7 AM on a freezing Monday morning in February 2012. I'm in a rented 2-bedroom flat just west of London.

I'm sitting on a hard wooden dining chair in front of my laptop, nursing a black coffee. The sound of the morning traffic is building below. But today is different because today I'm not heading out to join it. It's my first day as a self-employed entrepreneur. My one thought is, *"I have to make this work!"*

My grand plan was to sell SMS text marketing services to local businesses. Which, in hindsight, was a great idea that nobody knew they even needed.

As the weeks slipped past, my cash reserves dwindled. Rent day was looming. My then girlfriend (now wife) gave me that withered sidelong look. The one that says, *"When are you going to stop messing around and get a real job?"*

Drastic action was needed - one final roll of the dice. I put on a suit and walked around shops in local towns, asking shop owners if they would like to talk to me about SMS text messaging.

One Tuesday, I walked into a hair salon and spoke to the salon owner. I asked if he had a system to follow up with customers by text.

"No, thank you," he told me curtly, "My accountant deals with all my taxes."

"No, not *taxes*," I clarified. "*Text messaging*. Like on your phone."

"Oh, I don't think I need that," he replied after a pause. "But can you get me ranked on Google? You know, in the Google rankings?"

With all the nonchalance I could muster, I said, "I probably could". It wasn't the project I had set out to find, but client No.1 was finally on board!

Every business has a genesis story. New potential customers always ask themselves: are you trustworthy? Are you the expert you claim to be? How did you get to where you are today?

You have an opportunity to tell a slice of your story when potential customers enter your world. Not your whole story - just a slice. You get to pick a path through the jungle of your past. Your goals in doing this are threefold:

- To entertain
- To educate
- To upgrade your prospect's level of thinking about your topic.

Those are my goals for this chapter. First and foremost, to entertain you - because you won't remember the message if you're bored. Secondly, to educate you about business storytelling. Thirdly to elevate storytelling as a priority by stating the business case.

After working with the salon, I ran my own Google Ads to generate leads. When people searched for 'Google AdWords' and similar phrases, they would see my ad: (in 2012, it was still possible to bid on keywords like 'google adwords')

The ad offered a free report called '*How to Waste £1000 on Google AdWords in No Time Flat*'. When people registered, I sent them the report and added them to an automated fourteen-part email sequence. Over fourteen emails, I told parts of my story. Firstly, I told my readers how I got into Google AdWords (including the hair salon debacle).

I noticed I was getting two types of enquiries.

The first enquiries were from people who had stumbled across my website and wanted to know how much I charged. I remember taking a call from a guy who couldn't believe I didn't have a standard hourly rate! I closed a few of these deals, but often they were troublesome clients to work with. Usually, they were 'agency hoppers' who moved on after a traumatic month or two.

The second was people who had downloaded the report, read my emails and decided to contact me. These people were respectful of my time and less price sensitive. More than one said they felt they already 'knew me', even though we had previously never spoken. There was less pressure on the sales conversation; trust had already been established. Usually, the calls were to simply scope out the details of the project. The email series had already done the 'selling'.

A year later, I had built a small portfolio of AdWords clients. I noticed that two of my most sophisticated clients were using the CRM system Infusionsoft. These clients took marketing follow-up the most seriously and did the best job of following up with the leads I generated for them.

One was a company that trained mountain guides. Over four years, they took students to places like Patagonia, Alaska and Northern Spain and taught them to become mountain guides. The total tuition cost was around $100,000. Perhaps today, this is comparable to a university education, but it was a significant investment.

To generate leads, the company ran Google Ads (which was my job). When people opted in, we added them to an email sequence in Infusionsoft. The email sequence told stories. Stories from the founders and past students. Stories of harsh reality from the mountain top, such as terrifying blizzards. Other stories illustrated the leadership qualities of a good mountain leader.

In these emails, the call to action was to enter an application process, but the stories did the selling. The stories weren't superficial icing on the marketing cake. They were integral to the client education process. They were the foundation that supported everything else.

The Business Case for Storytelling

For the right business storytelling can be a business growth lever. A lever that, when pulled, takes your business from one level to the next. It does this by transforming the pre-sales experience, allowing your authentic self and real expertise to be seen. It also allows potential customers to get to know you without meeting you.

When you tell your story to a potential customer, you're replicating what would happen in a face to face meeting.

Let's say you meet a potential customer at a breakfast networking meeting. Your thirty-second pitch speaks to a problem they currently have. So you arrange a second meeting later in the week to discuss it over coffee.

This second meeting is the place to tell your story. If you didn't tell your story, it would be a very boring coffee! Or at least, a very transactional one.

Humans are natural storytellers. You tell stories automatically when face to face. You swim in a sea of stories all day long. We are simply attempting to replicate this online digitally. Your email marketing system replaces the coffee house. You're digitally replicating the coffee house conversation in your marketing emails.

Why Start with Emails?

It's best to tell your story first by email. Once you have a great email sequence, you can convert your stories into video and other formats. Email is the safest place to start telling your story because people have already opted in; at least in a fleeting way, they already 'know' you.

Start by identifying five to seven turning points in your career. I've told you two of mine in this chapter:

1. Meeting the hair salon owner and getting into Google Ads
2. Discovering the follow-up potential of Infusionsoft through my mountain training client

By reading those stories, you've traversed time and space to be with me. You've been a fly on the wall at two turning points in my career. You've walked a few steps in my shoes.

Five to seven turning points is a good rule of thumb because it gives you production options.

You can write a single email about each turning point, giving you a week-long email sequence. To extend the drama, you could write two emails about each turning point. For example, my story about the hair salon could be split into two emails: the first sharing my experience in the salon, the second talking about the project itself (which fell apart). They are the same story, but there are two separate 'theatres' of action.

This is how a seven-part sequence can become fifteen emails. With fifteen emails, you can send an email a day for just over two weeks. You can send an email every weekday for three weeks. Or you can send an email every other day for a month. The trust you build with new subscribers by doing this can support your business for years into the future.

Each email should focus on a specific point in time rather than a period of time. As Matthew Dick explains in his book *Storyworthy*, every great story contains a central five-second moment of character change.

In the hair salon, my five-second moment came when the salon owner said, "Oh, I don't think I need that, but can you get me ranked on Google." That was the five seconds where internally I thought, "Aaahhhhhh, *that's* what I need to do!"

Sharing these five-second moments is how you upgrade your reader's understanding of your topic. Those moments illustrate a specific point in time where you learned something profound about yourself that would be useful to a potential customer. You're using the story to shine light on an insight your customer may have missed. Sharing that insight both educates and builds trust.

Once you've got a great email sequence in place, you can repurpose your stories into other formats. You can tell stories anywhere you already have somebody's attention. This could be on a webinar, on stage, in direct mail, face-to-face, and on social media. Even in a book, like this one!

By doing this, you create a 6 Star experience for potential customers - by letting them get to know the real you.

Summary

Your story showcases the people behind your brand. Ultimately people still buy from people. It gives your marketing a personal touch.

Telling your story magnetically communicates your values. You will draw people who resonate with those values towards you. People who don't will unsubscribe. You're creating a 6 Star pre-sales experience for your *ideal* customer, not for your nightmare customer!

For the right business storytelling is a lever that can take your business from one level to the next. Storytelling can have a tangible impact on earnings per name, email engagement, email unsubscribe rates, even email deliverability. A good story sequence is a salesperson that never sleeps; entertaining and educating new prospects as they enter your world.

Humans have always told stories and always will. Therefore, you are communicating in a natural, authentic way by doing this. Because of this, stories DO belong in a business setting.

In your stories, you don't have to announce that you are telling a story. Instead, the reader should read the story as an interesting communication from a potential business supplier they are beginning to know, like and trust.

I wish you every success with your efforts.

ABOUT THE AUTHOR

ROB DRUMMOND, Founder, Story
Copywriters

Rob Drummond lives in Sheffield, England. Among other things, Rob is a copywriter, consultant, coffee snob, podcast listener, craft beer drinker, barefoot runner, father of two, lover of books, cricket fan, dark chocolate addict, and long-suffering supporter of Tranmere Rovers football club.

Rob is the founder of Story Copywriters, an online business that teaches marketers to write stories that sell. Learn more about Rob's work, book and podcast at:

https://www.storycopywriters.com/6star

CHAPTER EIGHTEEN

PROTECTING BUSINESSES' WEBSITE TRAFFIC - A NEW PARADIGM

'Prevention is better than cure'
~ Desiderius Erasmus 1500

2009-11 were tough years for me. When the world economy went into recession (The GFC), I found myself in 'Georgie's Financial Crisis' – my personal financial disaster!

One month before the financial crisis hit the mortgage industry in Australia, I got a job as a mortgage broker. Talk about timing! I owned four mortgaged properties, and this job was going to increase my income from previous years. Or at least that was the plan. I wanted to "retire" early and spend the rest of my life making money to help others.

However, over the next eight months, I earned about 50% of what I made in my previous job as a sales rep.

The mortgage franchise owner had to let me go. I was unemployed, with $6000 of expenses a month (rents did not cover the mortgages) and over $1 million in debt. I could not get any Centrelink income as I owned property (which is not easy to sell in a GFC). So I decided to move out of my house and rent it. I house-sat for strangers, looking after their pets in exchange for free housing. I moved on average every two weeks for the next six months until I moved in with my brother rent-free for six months in the storage area of his house.

I spent all day, every day, applying for jobs, which was more challenging than actually doing a job. If it had not been for the banks letting me put a hold on my mortgage payments, eventually selling three properties for less than I bought them, and my parents lending me $30,000, I would have been bankrupt and homeless in the streets.

It was a massive wake-up call that completely changed the trajectory of my life. Life had been easy up to that point, so I had taken enormous risks with no contingency plan. In hindsight, as horrible as it was, the truth is being at rock bottom, and almost homeless made me realise I could survive with almost nothing. It gave me the freedom to let go of all the things that didn't serve me in my life and only do what I was genuinely drawn to. But that didn't happen overnight; it was a long and sometimes painful road.

I started an Internet Marketing course, and finally, someone gave me a chance to do SEO (search engine optimisation) for them from home.

I knew nothing about business or getting clients. I needed them faster than what it would take to do SEO on my website. A mentor of mine explained the value of regularly attending a business breakfast. They told me that my clients would not come from the people at the breakfast but from the people they knew.

I went to a business breakfast for four years every Wednesday morning, even though I'm not a morning person. I built my business through referrals year on year. It's six years since I left the business breakfast, and over those six years, I have received enough referrals from my partners that it's the only marketing I needed.

2020/21 have been my best years so far. Luckily, I had chosen to work with clients who did incredibly well in the pandemic.

After what happened to me ten years ago, I now really feel for those struggling through this difficult time. I know what it's like to lose financially. To lose the things you were dreaming of having or doing. To not be anywhere near where you thought you were going to be.

I wanted to help and give back, so in 2020 I created a free online SEO course for business owners. I have also written seven SEO books, including step-by-step instructions of everything we do for our clients, for under $10.

My business was going well, but something else was troubling me.

A Massive Issue Needing a New Paradigm

Before the pandemic, I decided to write a book to help bring awareness and attempt to solve a big issue in web redevelopment - a possibility for all businesses involved in website redevelopment to provide a 6 Star service for their clients.

With ten years of experience in any industry, you become aware of the most common failure points. What doesn't work but is accepted maybe because we don't know how to change it. It might seem too overwhelming to change, or we think, "Who am I to try to change it?"

For two years or so, I sat around knowing things needed to change, hoping somebody else in the SEO industry might take the lead. But it didn't happen.

My mission is to raise awareness about this critical issue because I don't want business owners to go through the kind of financial disaster that I went through, especially when it's completely avoidable.

So, what needs to change? What am I talking about? How can all parties be 6 Star businesses?

I have coined the term '**SEO shielding**'.

Let me tell you a story

Michael has a business in the home-improvement industry, with a website that brings him 90% of the business's leads. So he decides to invest in a new website to get even more leads and trusts the web designer, who promises Michael it will work and claims he knows how to keep his current traffic!

About three months after his redesign has gone live, the phone stops ringing, and the business is no longer getting email inquiries from the website. Michael starts to worry. He looks at his rankings in Google and can't find them. He calls the web developer, who says that's okay - the traffic will go down, but then it will come back up again.

Now Michael is in a major panic. Does the web developer know what they're doing? How long is it going to take for the traffic to come back? Michael knows his business can only survive another two months without any leads.

At home, his wife is worried about him because she's never seen him so stressed. Michael is concerned about the seven staff he feels responsible for and their families. They're all relying on him and being able to provide for them is important to him.

He reaches out to other business owners and business coaches he knows to see if anyone can help.

That's when Michael was directed to me. I looked at his website and the Google archive of his old website and informed him that the SEO was not transferred across to the new site. Even if I start working on the site immediately, it could still take three or four months to get the traffic back.

Michael's new website, which was supposed to improve his business by bringing him more leads, has done the opposite - and halved his business for at least six months.

The frustrating thing for the SEO person (like me) who recovers the traffic for all the Michaels out there is it never needed to happen. If only business owners and web developers understood the risks are different for every website. If only a simple way existed for them to tell the risks and get an SEO migration specialist when needed, they could maintain the traffic and leads. Then the new website design can do what it's supposed to do, increase conversions.

There is no point in having a new, better converting website if there is no traffic to convert!

What do I want to change?

1. The lack of understanding that some websites and businesses are in massive danger in a website redesign, how to test for this, and the value of involving an experienced SEO consultant before the new website goes live.
2. The belief that you will lose a little bit of traffic, but it will just come back (magically).

3. The belief that all you need to do is some 301 redirects and install the SEO plugin. It is so much more than this!
4. The perception that changing the website design will always increase conversions. You can't increase conversions if traffic declines. You need both.

I want to create a new paradigm in which everyone knows how to check a website to see if it needs SEO Shielding. "**Prevention is better than cure**", and the cost businesses might incur to recover a website can be catastrophic compared to the cost of shielding.

Unless awareness is raised around this issue, business owners will continue to lose traffic and get the exact opposite of what they wanted with their website redesign. In the worst case, they will go bankrupt if it takes them too long to realise what has happened, and it proves impossible to get the traffic back fast enough for them to survive. As a Six Star business, we would not allow this to happen.

What Can a Business Owner do Right Now?

The first thing is to get Google Analytics installed on your website for at least two weeks. If you have months or years of data, even better. Then go into the "Acquisition" section, which shows where all your traffic is coming from at the time of writing. It should look like this image.

			Sessions ↓
▸ ▦ Customisation			
REPORTS			
▸ 🕐 Real-time			**52,099** % of Total: 100.00% (52,099)
▸ 👤 Audience			
▾ ⤨ Acquisition	☐	1. Organic Search	**39,395** (75.62%)
Overview	☐	2. Direct	**5,039** (9.67%)
▾ All Traffic	☐	3. Display	**3,744** (7.19%)
Channels	☐	4. Social	**1,453** (2.79%)
Treemaps	☐	5. Paid Search	**1,307** (2.51%)

Look at the percentage of traffic coming from Organic Search and from Direct Traffic (some of this can be organic). In this example, 75.62% is Organic Search from Google and other search engines.

If you are only getting 5% of your traffic from Organic Search and lose 50% of this with a website redesign, you're only going to lose 2.5%. That's not going to be a big problem unless you are a huge brand and 5% of your traffic is 50,000 hits a month.

However, if 50-90% of your traffic is coming from organic traffic and you lose 50% of it, how many leads a month would you lose? Could your business survive?

If you are tech-savvy and you feel completely comfortable going into your Google Analytics and checking this out, go for it. Otherwise, find an SEO consultant who specialises in SEO migration (shielding and recovery). Do a Zoom call with them and get them to show you where the traffic is coming from on your website to see the risks.

In Summary

Check your website to see how much Organic Search traffic you get and, therefore, how much danger your business is in with a redesign. Then, if required, find a Six Star business to manage this for you with a very experienced SEO specialist in SEO Migration (shielding and recovery). Then when the new site goes live, it does what it is supposed to do and brings you more leads so you can be the 6 Star business of your dreams!

ABOUT THE AUTHOR

GEORGIE HOPE

Georgie travelled to over 20 countries in her 20's and 30's. She was born and currently lives in Australia but spent nine years living in the UK. She is an INTP in the Myers Briggs and 9 in the enneagram. She loves animals and currently has two cats.

Georgie is passionate about protecting local businesses so they can continue to support their families, staff, and their community. She is the owner of Large Hope SEO, specialising in SEO Shielding and Recovery for local business websites and online stores built in WordPress. However, she is happy to speak to anyone with any type of website and direct them to someone who can help. Find out more here https://www.largehope.com/seo or email at info@largehope.com.

CHAPTER NINETEEN

HOW TO BECOME A 6 STAR COLLABORATOR

In 2008 I was working as a digital marketing consultant. At the time, a client asked whether I could drive traffic to their website. "I could, but it won't convert," I said honestly. "It's a waste of money."

"Well, can you do something about my website?" the client replied.

At that moment, a light bulb lit up in my brain. Yes, I *could... strategically*. But I couldn't do it technically as I was not a techie. So, I partnered with a technical web development application development business that could do the bits I couldn't - and do them well.

At the same time, I also worked with a woman with a print brand agency. Some of her clients were asking whether she could also do websites and digital work. She didn't know where to start, so I partnered with her on the digital side.

We worked together like this for a couple of years until I realised, "Why don't we just come together as one business?" So, we formalised our loose partnership and formed *BeSeen Marketing*, providing an end-to-end service proposition within one business. And again, the result was bigger than anything we could deliver by ourselves.

We already understood that we could work together and had already built a level of trust. When we came together as a business, we weren't forming new relationships. We knew it would work. Unbeknownst to me, I had created a real-world example of a 6 Star collaboration.

6 Star Collaboration Starts with Mindset

So many people find it challenging to work with others. Why is this? I've experienced 6 Star collaboration at all sizes of companies, from large corporations such as HP and Microsoft to many small businesses. I've discovered that 6 Star Collaboration reaps enormous dividends, the type of rewards that will contribute to making a 6 Star Business.

Many elements contribute to 6 Star Collaboration; however, it all starts with mindset. By mindset, I mean the willingness to work with others, be open and honest, explore and discover shared purpose, look for a win-win, and be positive.

Thomas Power calls this 'network thinking' which is Open, Random and Supportive (ORS), as opposed to institutional thinking, which is Closed, Selective and Controlling (CSC). To me, network thinking is collaborative thinking.

An institutional or rather a competitive mindset is very closed and limited to new opportunities. A competitive mindset is based on scarcity. By comparison, a collaborative mindset is based on abundance, opportunity and belief in a positive outcome.

Ask the Right Question

Collaboration is important. To achieve great things, you can't do everything yourself.

When presented with a problem, people tend to ask: "how am I going to solve this?" Which is the wrong question. The right question is, "**who** is going to solve this?"

You might well be doing too many things in your business. There may be many things that don't play to your strengths or can be fulfilled better elsewhere.

Collaboration can be a loose arrangement, like the consulting work that was a precursor to my agency. Or it could be a full-blown, formalised strategic partnership. You may even benefit from collaborating with who you perceive to be your 'competitors'!

Find your Community

To facilitate 6 Star collaboration, you first need to find the right environment and place to belong. Finding a suitable space where you can mix with like-minded people is vital for discovering collaboration opportunities.

In my current business Agency Local, we have created a community for the marketing and creative agency sector, including many web developers, brand designers, digital marketing agencies, copywriters etc. We create an environment where they get to know each other, learn from each other, discover each other's specialities and support each other.

Collaboration opportunities naturally appear as you get to 'know', 'like' and 'trust' one another. This is not the focus of Agency Local; however, collaboration is a natural by-product.

At Agency Local, we create an environment that helps facilitate collaboration in several different ways. First, we have an online community environment where people can ask questions and provide help and support. For example, I've recently seen people ask for bookkeeper recommendations. I've seen people ask tax questions. Because of the environment we've created, people immediately jump in with answers.

We also run 'Huddles', a way to meet and get to know other people. This creates an environment for people to get to know each other and build trust. It all constructs an environment that supports collaboration.

There isn't a correct environment for everyone, but there will be a collaborative environment out there that can support you and move you towards your goals.

Get Clear on Who You Serve

Having a niche or specialism makes collaboration so much easier. Specialism can be by sector, business size, specialist services, or by geography. For example, you could have two businesses that focus on digital paid advertising. Are they really competitors?

If one focuses on Facebook ads and the other on Instagram ads, then **no**.

If they both focus on Facebook and Instagram ads, but one focuses on hospitality clients and one on professional services clients, then **no**.

If one operates in the northern region and one in the south, then **no**.

If one suddenly gets too much work and needs to offload some to a safe pair of hands, then **no**!

Before collaboration opportunities arise, there is a necessary period of discovery that needs to take place. Understanding each other's businesses will lead to opportunities where businesses can fill gaps or enhance propositions.

The more niche and specific the audience you serve, the easier it is to collaborate.

Be Vulnerable

Vulnerability is a key element of the 6 Star collaboration. Discovery can only happen if you are vulnerable, which means being honest and open about the challenges you are facing.

If you share a challenge, you'll either find:

1. Other people who also have that challenge, which, in itself, can be therapeutic.
2. Other people who had the problem and can offer you specific advice to solve it.
3. Somebody who can take the problem off your hands!

The more open you can be about your challenges, the easier it is to collaborate. It's hard to collaborate with somebody who is a closed book.

Be Open to Opportunities

6 Star collaboration is about being open to opportunities, even from unexpected or unusual sources. You're trying to find the win-win in any social situation, rather than seeking the upside just for

yourself. Think: what will the other party gain from the collaboration? It's about having the creativity to explore new ideas. It's about building on whatever it is that somebody else is proposing.

Proactively Build Trust

Successful collaboration is built on a foundation of trust. You can't have any sort of collaboration without being able to trust the other party. Trust is built on two ingredients, competence and character.

Competence demonstrates that you can easily do what you say you'll do and do it to a high standard - it's simply your expertise. Although competence is relatively commonplace, and perhaps a '5 Star' ingredient, not 6 Stars.

Having character is more challenging and is where trust is built. Character is about being open and honest, being reliable and being a trustworthy person. Character is also about reciprocity, giving without expecting to receive and giving without an agenda. When you give unconditionally, you'll find that eventually comes back in bucket loads.

Trust takes time to build and seconds to destroy.

There is no accurate measure of trust; often, the most reliable measure is gut feel. What does your gut say about somebody? Trust your gut - it rarely lies!

Agree on a Common Purpose

Trust builds relationships. Collaboration is all about relationships. For effective 6 Star collaborations, relationships are based on a common purpose. Establishing a 'common purpose' means having mutual direction and desire to achieve a common outcome.

This motivates collaborations to succeed.

If you have shared goals towards a common purpose that makes collaboration easier, it reduces friction and accelerates momentum.

6 Star Collaboration Takes Work

You have to work at keeping and maintaining relationships. Loose collaborations are hard to keep going. And you need to be aware that people's priorities change.

Successful collaboration is a virtuous circle or positive feedback loop. Proactive and productive collaboration leads to more collaboration. If you have collaborated proactively with someone in the past, they are more likely to find opportunities for you in the future. Eventually, they may become an advocate for your business. People who know, like and trust you will be your best advocates.

You have to work consistently at building and then keeping and maintaining relationships! So when you find your community - work at it, turn up, contribute and engage. And when you find that relationship that may lead to opportunity, work at developing it.

You're looking for quality relationships, not quantity. So nurture and invest in the relationships that will move you forward. Dunbar's Number says that you can only maintain 150 relationships simultaneously, so be selective and work at the relationship.

Collaboration is discussion and exploration and working out what you can do together.

Create a Bigger Outcome by Working Together

How can collaboration work in practice? Just recently, I saw an Agency Local member respond to a large government tender. They quickly put together a whole team from our community to make a combined proposal.

We've got another member who runs a small boutique marketing agency. They're working hand in hand with a strategic marketer. One person does the strategy; the other does the implementation. It's a seamless end to end solution for the client, and it's based on strong collaboration between independent service providers who create a much bigger outcome by working together.

The outcome is greater than the sum of the parts because everyone focuses on their highest-value work.

Summary

Becoming a 6 Star collaborator starts with mindset. "WHO should do this?" is a better question than, "What do I need to do?"

Start by focusing on your ideal customer and your preferred line of work. Then, do only the work that you are uniquely positioned to do. Finally, pass everything else on to others.

6 Star collaboration requires you to be vulnerable. It requires you to give unconditionally. It requires work. It requires more than just staying in touch and involves conversation and exploration. Maintaining relationships for 6 Star collaboration is a two-way street, not a one-way broadcast.

More than anything, it starts with finding the right environment where you can meet others, establish trust and build relationships - and only then will 6 Star collaboration opportunities be born.

CHRIS BANTOCK

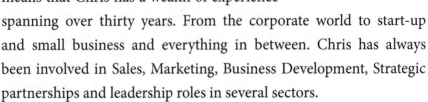

Being older than he cares to admit means that Chris has a wealth of experience spanning over thirty years. From the corporate world to start-up and small business and everything in between. Chris has always been involved in Sales, Marketing, Business Development, Strategic partnerships and leadership roles in several sectors.

After growing a Marketing agency over 12 years and successfully selling the business in 2018, Chris now dedicates his time to coaching and mentoring marketing agency owners to grow and develop their business and themselves as leaders.

Founded Agency Local in 2019 as a 'development community' for the marketing and creative sector where agency owners feel they belong, can get support and find collaborative opportunities. This enables Chris to follow his passion for helping people and businesses develop, create well run agency businesses, and achieve the life they deserve.

You can reach Chris via:

chris@agencylocal.co.uk

https://www.linkedin.com/in/chrisbantock/

www.agencylocal.co.uk

CHAPTER TWENTY

I've been in consulting for twenty years. Early in my consulting career, we believed there were two dominant cultures you might find within an organisation:

- A compliance-based culture, or
- A commitment-based culture

With compliance-based cultures, the assumption is that people are extrinsically motivated to get the job done and aim towards tangible things. Whereas commitment-based cultures assume people are intrinsically motivated. We used to expect the organisation's dominant culture would be one or the other. But, I now believe there is a third type of culture, a **purpose-driven culture**.

Over the last ten years, purpose-driven culture has become much more important. Think about the Teslas of this world. Everyone in these companies lives and breathe the same purpose. They are mission-based organisations; everyone is absolutely clear on the purpose of the organisation.

We've seen that a purpose-driven culture is considered the most desirable by employees, so many top-quality, highly skilled people will only apply to purpose-driven organisations whose values align with what they stand for.

This starts at the top with the founder's beliefs and values. The founder is always visible and vocal about the purpose of the organisation. For example, the culture at Tesla starts with Elon Musk. If you don't like what Elon says, you aren't going to work for Tesla!

Culture Eats Strategy for Breakfast

Entrepreneurs and senior business leaders spend a lot of time thinking about strategy. But if you're not deliberate and intentional about culture, your strategy will never be consistent over the long term.

I call this the 'cat's shiny light principle'. What do cats do? They follow a shining light wherever it goes. A lot of organisations are exactly like that and make many strategic decisions to maximise short-term revenue. This creates a short-term impact, but it's confusing for customers and employees. Employees lose sight of what you stand for and what impact you want to make in the world and begin to see themselves as a cog in the machine, a greaser of your bank account.

You can guide organisational culture, but your people create it. You can't be everywhere at once, so it's much better to attract individuals into your organisation who share your values.

The Three Secrets to a Strong Organisational Culture

I have found there are three components to creating a 6 Star organisational culture:

1. Enable the maximum potential of your employees.
2. Improve performance and hold people accountable.
3. Make your employees feel safe.

Start by identifying your value proposition. What do you stand for? What impact are you trying to make in the world?

You then need to enable potential within the organisation and create an environment that supports and encourages people to act in accordance with these values.

Finally, you need to provide a safe and stable environment in which people want to work. You need to give people the opportunity to align themselves with what your organisation stands for.

Make sure continuous improvement sits at the heart of your culture, as people need to see that what they're doing positively impacts work, colleagues, and the organisation.

Example - Alternative Energy

I worked with a client who described themselves as an alternative energy company. Essentially they're a waste management recycling organisation. They combine highly technological elements with the raw sifting and sorting of trash!

The leadership team wanted to make a visible, positive impact on the world, so we made some strategic changes.

One fundamental change was to implement a cradle-to-cradle recycling process. They now convert the initial plastic waste into usable plastics and manufacture new bottles and other products in their affiliated manufacturing sites.

Every landfill site now has targets to increase the percentage of materials recycled, and the amount of waste going to landfill has fallen sharply.

Now they've gone from being a waste management organisation to a cradle-to-cradle recycling organisation with a positive impact on world sustainability.

Within the organisational culture, we had to ensure that people aligned with those values and with the organisation's beliefs. So we started first with the organisation's purpose and made sure everyone knew what this purpose was. Then we developed a strategy in line with this purpose.

Purpose is critically important to the success of this company. Who grows up wanting to punch the clock for a waste management organisation? So we had to create a purpose that was bigger than the mechanics of the business.

It's still not the greatest environment to work in as there are implicit elements of the job which remain dirty and relatively risky, but they are making significant progress. These changes take time. But we've seen that employees want to align with the newly defined purpose. They see it as a badge of honour and talk highly about their employer purely because of what they can achieve, not what they accomplished in the past.

Culture Drives Business Longevity

How much do you think Elon Musk is driven by what his shareholders want? I'd say not very much in the short term.

Jeff Bezos was famous for this attitude in the early years of Amazon. Shareholders wanted to raise prices and increase short term profits. Bezos held out, almost bankrupting Amazon in the process. But the company survived, and look where Amazon is today. Bezos stuck to his values, and I'd wager that Amazon will be around for a long time into the future.

Very few companies operate in this way - maybe less than 1%. So, I call the companies that seek to build a purpose-driven culture the 'One Percenters'.

A purpose-driven organisation still respects the wishes of shareholders. But values and purpose are paramount and not to be compromised, so a purpose-driven organisation doesn't change direction to chase a shiny light or increase dividends by 0.001%.

The companies that will still be around in 50 years will be purpose-driven. Very few will achieve this, and in my opinion, many are missing the boat. This short-term pressure is driven by investors and by some of the top business schools. The first question they teach you to ask is: what is your exit strategy?

I want to build a purpose-driven organisation. While profitability matters, I'm not in it for short term gain. I'm in it for a long-term impact doing work that benefits companies across multiple continents.

Fostering a purpose-driven culture will allow you to have a lasting impact on the world and attract the right talent to help you achieve that impact. If you're trying to attract the best talent and plan to sell the business in five years, that's a clear conflict of interest.

Where to Begin

A purpose-driven culture starts at the top with the boards and C-suite. But, without agreement and buy-in from everyone at the top, short term pressures will prevail.

Can you name a company where everybody at the organisation knows the values of the organisation? Or where everybody knows what the company stands for? Most wouldn't be able to tell you or would tell you a different story.

Everybody knows what Tesla wants to achieve. Becoming purpose-driven starts with being very clear on what you stand for.

After this, the following steps depend on organisational strategy, but we usually focus on training, coaching, and customer-driven consultancy activities. We start from the top of the organisation and work our way down. Change needs to be embedded from the top to create a pull model, not a push model. You can't push anything on anybody if you want it to be sustainable! Remember, culture is created by your people, not dictated by management.

How a Purpose-Driven Culture can go Wrong

The key pitfall is not defining a clear end goal you're striving for. Without a clear and established end goal, you can never end up in the right place.

Sometimes a poor strategic decision might cause a minimal divergence. No big deal, right? Nothing may happen for months, sometimes years even. Everybody may still be happy, but you're diverging away from your purpose. Over time, that divergence will widen to the point where people no longer associate with what the organisation stands for.

Sometimes an organisation will change their values as a cosmetic exercise. They'll hang the updated values on the wall and implement a communications strategy to inform everybody. Initially, it might be very successful. Everybody says, "Wow, that's great! The organisation really wants to take us places, and I'm 100% in." However, soon after the communication strategy is launched, it becomes clear that no actual changes are happening.

Over twenty years, I've found that organisations are too inward-looking or have no idea what a 6 Star purpose-driven culture looks like. We all lack perspective on the business, especially when you're in it every day. The risk is that you change values as a cosmetic exercise rather than delivering real environmental change.

A lot of organisations talk about having a continuous development culture. But if you look at the initiatives they're putting out for their people to grow and develop, it's very limited.

I'm not saying spend 10% of your revenue on people development. But you need to ensure you have a good variety of programs to enable your people and work with the assets you currently have within your organisation.

For example, in my business, we've built an online mentoring system to enable individuals and organisations to have highly effective mentoring relationships inside and outside of their organisation. Mentoring as an effective, value-adding programme is relatively low cost. But, you're maximising the employee engagement and experience, maximising the knowledge you have internally and passing that on to the younger generation. You're creating a culture of care for each other, enabling potential long into the future.

How Long Does it Take to Build a Purpose-Driven Culture?

To truly transform the organisation's culture, we work with organisations for between six months and three years. Of course, this isn't a 'quick fix', but it's a worthwhile one!

The actions we implement depend on the goal of the client and the current situation. The changes can come from a safety angle, a performance improvement angle, a potential enabling angle, or a combination of these. By making these changes, our goal is to have a lasting, sustainable impact on the organisations we work with. We're putting the right stepping stones in place for long-term, purpose-driven success. We want our clients to achieve and sustain this long after we're gone.

That's my wish for you too.

Get clear on your values. Communicate your values. Make sure everyone at the top of your company knows what your values are. Then support and enable your employees to deliver on those values and start putting the right building blocks in place to achieve your new purpose-driven vision.

ABOUT THE AUTHOR

DAVE VRIJSEN

Dave is the Founder & CEO of Sageflow. He is a seasoned CEO and Business Owner who has established a multinational business based on targeted customer pains and needs. Therefore, it was vital to him to develop a business that was completely aligned with his own values and beliefs and develop deep and lasting relationships with people who share this same approach in both business & life.

Dave has a truly international character, which is represented in his family structure, whereby every member of his family has been born in a different country. He has now settled in Brisbane, Australia, together with his family, and continues to live by his outstanding values and beliefs and strives for excellence in everything he and his company does.

You can reach Dave via:

W: sageflow.com.au

LI: linkedin.com/in/davevrijsen

CHAPTER TWENTY ONE

"I hate the idea that business leaders could be held accountable for the culture of their organisations! If people don't like it, they can get out and make way for someone else!"

So said – or rather shouted – a CEO to me during a recent conversation in which a Chief Risk Officer of a large organisation shared his views of the increasing risk to leadership teams of legal liability for toxic workplace cultures. There have been test cases already in some jurisdictions, and the recently-launched ISO45003 framework for psychological wellbeing at work opens the prospect of greater accountability (as well as guiding improvement!).

His was perhaps an extreme view – but not a unique one in the contemporary leadership narrative. That strikes me as truly bizarre. In an environment where the ability to solve complex problems with creative, innovative solutions created in collaboration with people from diverse backgrounds, experience and locations, shouldn't it be the responsibility of organisational leaders to create and sustain cultures conducive to those qualities?

I contend that the 6 Star businesses we envisage will accept, embrace and practice exactly that premise, and reap performance, reputational and financial rewards in return.

Today, discussion on wellbeing at work is contextualised by the Covid-19 pandemic and its impact on how and where we work and how we frame the future of work.

But the relationship between work and human wellbeing did not arise with the pandemic. Much sobering data on the impact work has on health and wellbeing has existed for years; it has proven convenient or expedient to ignore it.

The pandemic has put the data in context, particularly in an environment where the digital transformation of business is inevitable and accelerating. And the appeal of greater flexibility in the physical location of the workplace, for both employers and employees, has soared. This sets a useful context from which to explore this topic.

Our own research on the impact of working from home suggests three important findings:

1. Initially, working from home brought freedom, flexibility and the ability to focus without the usual workplace distractions and interference.

2. This quickly gave way to the negative aspects of social isolation and loneliness, feeling disconnected from the organisational dialogue and the absence of the chance conversations that spark new ideas on addressing challenging problems or progressing new opportunities.

3. Finally, and when it looked like working from home might become a long-term proposition with the appeal to employers of reducing commercial real-estate costs, the imposition of manufacturing-era 'scientific management' practices effectively destroyed all the benefits experienced in the initial stage.

These practices, from checking log-on times and measuring response times to messages to the most pernicious of all, using remote-worker tracking software, are experienced by employees as surveillance and intrusive micro-management. This completely removes the boundary between work and non-work and increases anxiety and stress levels. And in turn, effectively suppressing creativity and other higher-order cognitive tasks fundamental to knowledge work and is unquestionably detrimental to wellbeing in the context of work, if not the workplace itself, in a traditional sense.

What can we draw from this?

First, it underscores the misalignment between traditional notions of 'productivity' as a measure of employee value and the realities of knowledge work.

Measuring what time people logged on; how much time they spent at their keyboard, and how often they took 'breaks' (evidenced by the cessation of keystrokes) is entirely out of sync with the kind of work that should be the most valuable and productive use of their time, talent and connections with others within and beyond their companies.

This points to the importance of social connection as a component of performance and employee wellbeing. Remove those from the experience of work, and wellbeing diminishes as a direct consequence.

A third conclusion, obvious but worth stating, is a causal relationship between work and human wellbeing. Work can be energising, engaging and conducive to wellbeing, or debilitating, depressing and detrimental to wellbeing.

Perhaps the most important conclusion is that wellbeing as a concept ultimately has at least a degree of subjectivity to it. For example, some people like working from home while others do not. Some people crave human connections in the office; others are happy to avoid them.

The ultimate judge of the state of wellbeing at work is the people who experience that work and how it affects them. We can certify buildings as LEED or WELL compliant according to objective standards – but we can't just 'tell' employees they work in an environment 'certified' for its positive impact on their wellbeing. They will be the judges of any wellbeing strategy.

The temptation is to see wellbeing as an 'umbrella', under which we deploy 'tactics' such as yoga classes or mindfulness seminars and lectures on stress management. This makes it look manageable, and someone can be given responsibility for it.

The challenge is that it assumes that elements outside the umbrella have no impact on the outcome. In the case of wellbeing, we know that isn't true. So rather than an umbrella view, we are better off taking wellbeing as a lens through which we see the entire organisation and the positive and negative impacts on the wellbeing of all elements.

So how might a 6 Star Business go about tackling this?

I think there are three considerations:

1. **The subjective element of wellbeing means an effective wellbeing strategy cannot be 'top-down'.**

We can't 'do wellbeing' to employees.Instead, we first need to understand:

- What employees think wellbeing at work is.
- What employees believe positively affects their wellbeing at work.
- What employees believe negatively affects their wellbeing at work.
- What they think their company could do to improve wellbeing at work.

Most attempts to assess workplace wellbeing through surveys tend to be framed around preconceptions about workplace wellbeing and, therefore, what questions to ask.

This 'institutionalises' the cognitive biases involved and easily leads to conclusions that don't adequately reflect the needs, interests or aspirations of the employees as key stakeholders.

We need to understand wellbeing from their experience, not a 'management depiction' of what we think it should mean.

2. Be deliberately inclusive in ownership of wellbeing strategy

I hear a frequent question in my work advising and guiding leadership teams in improving workplace wellbeing, which is, "Who 'owns' it?" This is a perfectly natural question in the traditional 'umbrella' way we have thought about areas of work with a responsible manager tasked with delivering specific outcomes using specific inputs in terms of financial, human and other resources.

That gets us into trouble when it comes to wellbeing and the interrelationships between the elements that affect wellbeing, cross-functional and other lines of control.

The solution is twofold:

- Give wellbeing prominence through having (at least) Management Board level sponsorship; and
- Be as deliberately inclusive as possible in involving employees in designing solution strategies. Address wellbeing with cross-functional, multi-generational teams, fully representative of all employee groups, forming a 'Wellbeing Board'. Do 'Diversity and Inclusion' by being diverse and inclusive, instead of treating it as a topic and talking about its importance.

The Wellbeing Board should have the mandate to turn the employee insights into practical experiments aimed at addressing and improving wellbeing – and again, involving employees themselves in designing and defining those experiments. Scale what works, cease what doesn't – rinse and repeat, with the Board sponsor providing top cover and negotiating the inevitable trade-offs among the leadership team.

3. Equip People Leaders to understand their role in terms of looking after the wellbeing of themselves and their teams as a core asset of organisational performance

There is substantial evidence that many employees see their line manager or supervisor as the primary source of workplace stress and ill-health. For example, Gallup and others have produced statistics suggesting that '65% of employees would take a pay-cut if it meant their boss would be sacked' or '70% of employees cite their boss as the biggest source of stress.'

Day-to-day interactions with line managers and other team members will inevitably have some material impact on wellbeing at work. But line managers have rarely been adequately prepared even to consider wellbeing as part of their remit. For example, in 2020, there were no MBA programs that paid any attention to it at all.

And I am not just talking about line managers addressing the wellbeing of their teams; they are all too frequently working on the limits of burnout without either recognising it or, if they do, knowing how to deal with it. This naturally is 'transmitted' through the emotional contagion effect to their team members, leading to poorer performance over time and exacerbating the underlying problem.

We need to equip *all* managers to understand the relationship between stress and performance, identify the sources of chronic and dysfunctional stress, and attend to the wellbeing of themselves and their teams as an integral part of their role and responsibility.

The challenge of workplace wellbeing is often described as an 'upstream' problem: the root cause rarely gets addressed until it produces symptoms and dysfunction that lead to crisis and the need for urgent attention.

I call it 'the gurney problem'. Being told to change your diet, exercise, substance use and stress management while you are on a gurney being wheeled into the emergency room during a heart attack is completely useless at that moment. The attendant issue is to stop you from dying, requiring specific medical and perhaps surgical interventions.

But here's the rub: If you had done these things earlier, you might not be here today – and (assuming we are successful in preventing you from dying today), you need to start doing these things from now on – or else you might be back here again and not be so lucky next time around.

In reality, many patients who have been in this situation still fail to take the necessary lifestyle actions that improve their cardiac health and longevity.

The most successful approaches start with understanding what is important from the patient's point of view (that might create a powerful enough reason to get them moving in a new direction and make changes). And to identify easily repeatable small steps to integrate into their life without too much difficulty; to reframe the shift from 'insurmountable challenge' to 'manageable and worthwhile goal'.

We can apply this same experience to workplace wellbeing. We have an opportunity now for the 'crisis' of the pandemic to be an inflexion point in the relationship between work, wellbeing and health.

The 6 Star Businesses of tomorrow will be those who do not waste this crisis; and help their employees *do* better, *feel* better and *stay* better at work.

ABOUT THE AUTHOR

GRAHAM BARKUS

Graham is a clinical coach-consultant with over 25 years of experience helping executives and organisations achieve and sustain peak performance. As an external coach/consultant and in senior organisation development roles he has led major change and development initiatives across Asia and globally.

His approach draw upon his background in coaching psychology, cognitive-behavioural therapies and dispute resolution, to help clients close the gap between 'resolve and results' and achieve better outcomes, faster.

Based in Hong Kong, Graham's experience has spanned diverse industries including aviation, banking and finance, biotech, engineering consultancy, FMCG, healthcare, insurance, logistics and real estate development. He frequently collaborates with top-tier universities – from business schools to medical schools - to bridge leading-edge theory and research to the real-world, real-time considerations of practice in diverse, multicultural markets.

Graham holds postgraduate degrees with distinctions in Clinical Organizational Psychology (INSEAD); Strategy & Innovation (University of Oxford), and an LLM in Arbitration and Dispute Resolution from the University of Hong Kong. He is master-certified in executive and integrative health coaching methodologies and is a Founding Fellow at the Institute of Coaching at Harvard University as well as being a member of the International Society for the Psychoanalytic Study of Organizations and the Australasian Society for Lifestyle Medicine.

CHAPTER TWENTY TWO

A UNIVERSAL GUIDE TO BEING (CONSCIOUS)

Your loving, your wellbeing,
and BEING a 6 Star business leader
– by Marti Spiegelman

How you stand here is important.
How you listen for the next things to come.
How you breathe.
– William Stafford, 'Being a Person'

A 6 STAR Business is a 'collectively conscious business' and a 6 STAR Business Leader is a 'collectively conscious' person – simple statements, but just definitions. Caution is advised when entering this kind of discussion – we often feel we've arrived the moment we have a definition, but then we're at risk of missing the experience altogether. Just 'doing conscious things' in business doesn't mean the business is functioning as an expression of universal consciousness, nor does it ignite the *experience of being* that lies at the source of becoming a collectively conscious 6 STAR Leader with a real 6 STAR Business.

Many people attempt to 'make' business conscious, but consciousness is not something we can declare or dictate – it is not a concept, an instruction, or a strategy. At the universal scale, it is a force – a flow of energy and information that gives rise to everything, visible and invisible. At the human scale, where we function as an expression of this universal flow, consciousness becomes an open-ended, creative state of *being* that is achieved through the mastery of outwardly connected awareness.

To approach this mastery, we must first set definitions aside and gain a little insight into our human way of 'being'.

When I was two years old, I discovered the experience of *being* at a universal scale. Every night before going to sleep, I remember trying to imagine my way to the edge of the universe. It was a vivid experience – I knew I was experiencing the journey directly – I sensed it, saw it, felt it, tasted it, heard the faint hiss of starlight.

'Everyone' (my understanding of adults at the time) said the universe had an edge, and as a small being just beginning to soak up the world and learning about edges of all kinds, why not find this one? Every night I found a membrane at the so-called edge of our universe – I recall pausing there, wondering what lay beyond. 'Everyone' had told me there's nothing beyond 'the edge', but I couldn't imagine nothing! So every night, I punched through the membrane and found more universe! – more stars, galaxies and planets, more light, energy, and possibility, stretching into infinity. This recurring discovery was the most reassuring and empowering experience ever – discovering something so constant and yet infinite, experiencing myself as part of something that both held and expanded me, knowing I could 'sense' my way there anytime.

But here's the real magic. I didn't end up 'there' – I wasn't lost in space. Instead, the depth of that connection and the 'response' I felt from the universe brought my young self 'here' where I felt held, grounded, supported, and, as I would realise later in life, loved by the universe itself.

This is an essential experience in developing full consciousness – being connected via your awareness into the world as a dynamic part of the world, informed by and responding to the world, participating in creating new aspects of that larger world. You begin to experience your body as part of the earth, your work as a creative 'node' in the larger natural systems of life, your awareness as an inextricable part of the universe. You begin contributing at evolutionary levels. You are no longer an individual person or organisation trying to think and do things better.

As I grew into adulthood, I noticed more and more that people around me didn't experience themselves as part of something bigger. 'Belonging' meant being *ex*clusive, not *in*clusive. They were more aware of being independent and 'above it all' – focused on declaring their uniqueness, 'owning' their ideas, and beating the competition. They concentrated on getting 'there' and seemed not to know where 'here' was. So many people seemed defended against the world yet wished it would recognise them as a Star. Instead of receiving information and energy from the world, they took their awareness inward, trying to think their way to solutions rather than risk the power of direct experiential knowing and creating.

I gradually realised that people in western culture have a habit of removing awareness from the world instead of allowing their awareness to connect them to it. When we lose our sensing connections into the world, we lose everything we need for thriving. We lose our capacity to receive nurturance, we lose community, we lose love and our ability to love, we lose the connected state of being that brings to us what we need for health and wellbeing.

Think of these connections as pathways of communication and exchange between you and the universe. Imagine yourself informed through these connections, receiving what you seek, allowing larger forces to guide and support you.

These pathways are what awareness uses to gather 'sensory data' in all dimensions, even beyond known horizons. This is what it means to perceive – to know the world through the senses. The sensory data we receive converges into evolutionary ideas, new meaning, and new value. This, in turn, ignites new choices and actions. This only occurs with well-connected awareness – you cannot think your way to it.

Outwardly-connected awareness in the 6 STAR Business Leader is the source of the 6 STAR Business capacity to be a conduit for the power of consciousness, bringing never-before-imagined products, services, and benefit into our world. To be a 6 STAR Business Leader is to be a change-maker – and to truly change the world, you must first change the way you *know* the world . . . by changing how you use awareness.

But the magic begins within you as a human being. When you learn how to connect your awareness to the world and focus it on discovery and precise creative action, you begin to BE different. You experience 'being' love, the love of the universe. This is accompanied by a profound sense of 'coming home' to yourself and belonging in life. You gradually realise you're experiencing a new dimension of wellbeing and your relationships become more compassionate and resilient. You become more present, fluid, and negotiable in all your interactions.

Your creative capacity takes quantum leaps in your work, and you discover new depths of possibility and value in your talents. You develop a new ability to draw resources, insights, and energy from seemingly invisible sources and use these to laser-focus your work in the world.

Instead of just 'working ahead of the curve', you become the maker of the curve. In this fully connected, experiential state, you can become the 'maker' of a 6 STAR Business.

The core of our being is the act of perception.
The magic of our being is the act of awareness.
– The Wheel of Time, Carlos Castaneda

Here's what graduates of the Precision Consciousness Training have to say:

I realise that the ability for connection is within myself, and the flow, the happiness, and freedom I feel are the result of that connection. My life, my work, and even my idea of work are much more expansive – this is living life in the universe.
– Greg Bernarda, Business Advisor, Switzerland

I really have started to see the world in an entirely different way, and I know I'm fully participating in life now – this is an incredible shift.
– Todd Hoskins, Business Advisor, US

The collective is much more real and alive for me, as is the sense of 'coming home'. I don't feel a weird outlier anymore; I feel a sense of belonging to something bigger, timeless, and exhilarating. At a practical level, I don't make decisions the way I used to – I'm much more in the moment and rely on the tools of Precision Consciousness to understand what's required, in real-time. That's absolutely liberating!
– Josie Gibson, Director, The Catalyst Network, Australia

In a world where the cult of the individual can isolate us and rob us of deeper meaning, the Precision Consciousness Training is the best antidote I know.
– Pia Kealey, Professional Author, US

These professionals have trained their awareness and worked with the 'Technologies of Precision Consciousness' – a set of organising principles that, when embodied, permanently wire us into the universe, inform us, and activate our creative roles in the greater system of life. These principles are akin to an 'original physics' – an encoding of how energy becomes matter in a conscious universe. When we embody these principles, full connectivity and presence become our nature. Unconditional love and acceptance become the basis of our membership in life. We seek out complementarities (we often say 'opposites') as creative resources. We invest in our relationships as sources of abundance, and collectivity becomes our way of increasing the value and positive impact of everyone's uniqueness.

This is just a taste of who we become when we master awareness, and 'Precision Consciousness' informs our way of being. It's the way of

6 STAR Leaders creating 6 STAR Businesses for our emerging world, and it's limitless.

Any technology sufficiently advanced is indistinguishable from magic.
– Arthur C. Clarke

It's a big moment when we finally experience our awareness at work. We usually think we're already aware, but that's the speed bmp right there – we're thinking, not experiencing. When we're thinking, we focus our awareness on thoughts, ideas, language, and linear maps of action, which are all *outcomes of our sensory experience*, not the direct experience itself. So, we have to train our awareness to engage the depth and precision of direct sensory experience – just as indigenous elders have trained countless generations of their children.

Start at the beginning – take your awareness off yourself and flow it into the world around you. Then try this essential exercise from indigenous cultures. As you explore the world with awareness, keep a notebook handy to capture every new idea, insight, and inspiration that arrives in your awareness because as you connect outwardly, the universe will begin delivering them to you.

• **BEING HERE** Find a beautiful spot in nature, a place where you can sit undisturbed for a while, preferably on the ground. Your task is to experience your surroundings through your senses, without thinking at all – no naming, no explanations in your head, no ego chatter distracting you. Put your awareness on the sights, sounds, scents, and textures around you. Experience the light and shadows, colours, humidity, movements, forms, and especially the energies of your entire surroundings. All without thinking. If you notice you're thinking, drop it and move your awareness outward again. Bring all the sensory detail into awareness, gradually increasing the radius of your connections. Find your place in the universe by letting it find you. Do this often.

ABOUT THE AUTHOR

MARTI SPIEGELMAN

Marti Spiegelman is a business advisor and mentor, speaker, and founder of *The Precision Consciousness Training: Technologies of Consciousness for Today's Leaders.*

Marti has combined five decades of business experience with her training in the sciences, graphic design, and indigenous technologies of consciousness to create a modern methodology for mastering full consciousness at all scales – individual, organizational, societal, and global.

Marti holds a BA in biochemistry from Harvard and an MFA in graphic design from Yale Design School. She also has advanced training in psychology, anthropology, and neurophysiology, and is initiated into indigenous lineages in Peru, West Africa, and the Himalayas. Marti serves as Director of Communications on the Board of the Andean Research Institute.

Marti has unique insights into how consciousness drives innovation and thriving in business, finance, and society. She brings the extraordinary principles of 'Precision Consciousness' to awakening leaders in all fields – the change-makers and visionaries who are striving to take business, community building, and creative endeavour to new levels of conscious success in our evolving world.

https://www.yourprecisionconsciousness.com

https://www.technologiesofconsciousness.com

https://www.leadingfrombeing.com/podcast

https://www.youtube.com/embed/AJBvMu2wJ5k

martispiegelman@mac.com | +1 415.722.5521

EPILOGUE

The path to a 6 Star Business is evolving, much like every other journey, we take.

There are surprises, twists, shocks, and discomfort. Yet all those experiences are required for us to evolve and morph into the new version of ourselves.

By adopting a practice of curiosity, we can begin to see the world differently in each moment we experience it. As Business Owners, we can be curious every day about what it takes to be 6 Star, and we believe it's what is inherently inside all of us naturally.

As this book ends, allow the next chapter of your evolution to open to all the possibilities of what it means for you to be '6 Star'.

Thanks for being on this journey with us; we're very grateful.

If you'd like to connect with us, please do so here:

Podcast: https://podcast.6star.business

Community: https://community.6star.business

We hope to meet with you in the near future.

Aveline & Pete

9 781637 922026